VOCAL CHAMBER MUSIC

GARLAND REFERENCE LIBRARY
OF THE HUMANITIES
(Vol. 465)

VOCAL CHAMBER MUSIC
A Performer's Guide

Kay Dunlap
Barbara Winchester

GARLAND PUBLISHING, INC. • NEW YORK & LONDON
1985

Library of Congress Cataloging-in-Publication Data

Dunlap, Kay, 1945–
  Vocal chamber music.

  (Garland reference library of the humanities ; v. 465).
  Includes index.
  1. Vocal music—Bibliography. I. Winchester, Barbara,
1943–   . II. Title. III. Series.
  ML128.V7D86 1985   016.7843′06   83-49309
  ISBN 0-8240-9003-9 (alk. paper)

Printed on acid-free, 250-year-life paper
Manufactured in the United States of America

To our husbands, Steven Solomon and Malcolm Peyton, who never stopped believing that this project would be completed.

CONTENTS

PREFACE

The extensive revival of chamber music in recent years has made its impact on singers everywhere: singers are becoming increasingly aware that there is a vast, diverse, and seldom-performed repertoire waiting to be discovered. The effects of this expanded interest have ranged from the inclusion of ensemble repertoire in the simple song recital for voice and piano, to the formation of new performing ensembles whose primary purpose is to perform vocal chamber music from the past, as well as to encourage the composition of new works.

The selection of ensemble repertoire for performance, always a difficult task, has been even more difficult for the singer. For most instrumentalists, the process is simplified by the use of one of the appropriate bibliographies at hand. Unfortunately, those for the voice deal mostly with works for a single voice and piano, or voice and one instrument, or family of instruments. There is no comprehensive source to aid the singer in surveying the complete repertoire.

This book is intended to be a practical guide for that purpose. In some cases, perhaps it will inspire the reprinting of works which have long been unavailable. Most of all, it will be a help to that ever increasing number of singers who find pleasure in such works.

CRITERIA

1. Works included are scored for at least one voice and one instrument (other
    than keyboard or guitar), up to twelve solo voices and twelve solo instru-
    ments in all. When there is a history of a work being performed by solo
    voices *or* chorus, the work has been included and the decision left to the
    performer.
2. The time span covered is approximately 1650 to 1980. Earlier works such as
    madrigals are not included because of the immense body of literature in-
    volved and its general availability in collections.
3. The majority of entries are those with English, French, German, Italian,
    Spanish, or Latin texts, but significant works in other languages or in
    translation have also been included.
4. In selecting composers, an attempt was made to include all major composers
    and to introduce other composers of merit whose works have been published.
    Whenever possible, the works included have been examined by the authors.
5. Most of the works listed are currently in print. Some works known to be
    out of print are included because of their musical interest (see the
    Guide to Use).
6. No arrangements are included except in those instances where the arrange-
    ment bears the unmistakable stamp of the **arranger's** style (see Beethoven,
    Berio, Haydn).
7. No excerpts from larger works are included. For example, there are no
    arias from Bach cantatas listed, even though many of them fit the scoring
    criteria.
8. When possible, all movements of cycles are listed, even when some of them
    do not fit the scoring criteria, since they were intended to be performed
    as a whole. A missing number in an opus indicates that the work does not
    fit the scoring criteria and that the piece may be performed separately,
    or that it is unpublished or unavailable.

GUIDE TO USE

Compers, opus, title, author. Entries are in alphabetical order by composer. Works are listed by opus number where applicable or in alphabetical order. Where only some of a composer's works have opus numbers, those without opus numbers are listed last in alphabetical order. The author of the text is given in parentheses following the title. Generally, the language of the title is the language of the text. When the text is in another language, or in more than one language, this is indicated in parentheses following the author's name. Comments are listed under the titles after an asterisk. They include timings when known, seasonal nature of the work, and other pertinent information.

Publication information. Where possible, a modern edition is listed for works also available in the complete works of a composer unless the complete works is more reliable or the modern edition is very difficult to obtain, as with Russian publishers. The dates listed are the most recent dates of publication and, therefore, not an accurate indication of the date of composition. In the case of out-of-print works, a library holding a score is listed along with the publisher (if it is still in business), since out of print works can sometimes be obtained by writing to the publisher. Consult the list of Music Sources for full names of libraries, publishers, and collections.

Scoring. Voices are listed first in score order, followed by instruments in alphabetical order. A parentheses indicates an alternate scoring, e.g., S(T) indicates that either a soprano or tenor may sing the work. When instruments are followed by a slash, this means the instrument plays all the instruments listed, e.g., fl/pic/afl means that the flutist also plays piccolo and alto flute.

Index. Works are indexed by scoring in the same format as those in the Guide.

ACKNOWLEDGMENTS

The authors are grateful to Raymond Beegle, John Moriarty, and Julia Sutton, who read the initial project description, to Geraldine Ostrove who introduced us to our publisher, to our editor Julia Johnson for her infinite patience, to Esther Breslau and Benjamin Sears of Yesterday Service, Inc., for their invaluable assistance in finding music and publication information, and to Chris Fujiwara who taught us the wonders of the computer.

ABBREVIATIONS

A	alto	db	double bass
acc	accordion	dif	difficult
acl	clarinet in A	dramS	dramatic soprano
afl	alto flute	Ebcl	clarinet in Eb
amp	amplified	elec db	electric double bass
anthol	anthology	elec gtr	electric guitar
arec	alto recorder	elec hpd	electric harpsichord
arr	arrangements	elec org	electric organ
asax	alto saxophone	elec pf	electric piano
auth	authorized	elec vc	electric cello
avail	available	eng hn	english horn
B	bass	fing cym	finger cymbals
ban	banjo	fl	flute
Bar	baritone	flug hn	flugelhorn
bas hn	basset horn	fV	female voice
Bbar	Bass-baritone	gam	viola da gamba
bc	basso continuo	glk	glockenspiel
bcl	bass clarinet	gtr	guitar
bfl	bass flute	harm	harmonium
bn	bassoon	hi	high
br	brass	hiS	high soprano
bS	boy soprano	hn	horn
bshn	bass horn	hnd	hand (bells)
btrbn	bass trombone	hp	harp
bviol	bass viol	hpd	harpsichord
cast	castenets	inst	instruments
cbn	contra-bassoon	kbd(s)	keyboard(s)
cem	cembalo	lowV	low voice
cel	celesta	mand	mandolin
chim	chimes	mar	marimba
cimb	cimbalom	medV	medium voice
cl	clarinet	mel	melody
colS	coloratura soprano	Ms	mezzo-soprano
comb	combination	mV	male voice
cor	cornet	nar	narrator
crot	crotales	ob	oboe
Ct	counter-tenor	obb	obbligato
cym	cymbals	ob d'am	oboe d'amore

opt	optional	tom	tomtom
org	organ	tp	tape
orig	originally	trbn	trombone
perc	percussion	treb	treble
pf	piano	trec	tenor recorder
pf 4hnds	piano four hands	tsax	tenor saxophone
pf qnt	piano quintet	ttrbn	tenor trombone
pf tr	piano trio	tpt	trumpet
pic	piccolo	trans	translation
prep	prepared (piano)	tub	tubular (bells)
rec	recorder	uk	ukelele
S	soprano	V	voice
sax	saxophone	va	viola
snare	snare drum	var	various
spkr	speaker	vc	cello
srec	soprano recorder	va d'am	viola d'amore
st	strings	vib	vibraphone
st qt	string quartet	vle	violone
st qnt	string quintet	vn	violin
st tr	string trio	ww	woodwinds
syn	synthesizer	ww qt	woodwind quartet
T	tenor	ww qnt	woodwind quintet
tam	tamtam	xyl	xylophone
timp	timpani		

Vocal Chamber Music

Opus, composer, title, text	published	scoring
ABBADO, MARCELLO (1926-)		
Cantata	Zerboni	fV, 6inst
Ciapo	"	fV, 9inst
15 Poesie T'ang * 21'	"	Ms, fl, pf, ob, vc
ABSIL, JEAN (1893-1974)		
12 5 Mélodies (Maeterlinck, Valéry, Hugo)	CeBeDeM	Ms, st qt(pf)
ADAM, ADOLPHE-CHARLES (1803-1856)		
Variations	Ricordi	S, fl, pf
AGER, KLAUS (1946-)		
Requiem	Modern	S, cl/bcl, fl/pic, pf, vc, vn
AHRENS, JOSEPH (1904-)		
Regnum Dei	Müller	B, bn, cl, eng hn, fl, hn, kbd, ob
AITKEN, HUGH (1924-)		
Cantata 1 (Elizabethan poets)	Oxford	T, ob, va, vc, vn
Cantata 2 (Rilke) (Ger/Eng) * 9-10'	"	T, db, fl/pic, ob, va, vc
Cantata 3 (Barnstone) * 13'	"	T, ob, va
Cantata 4 (Machado) (Sp)	"	S, db, fl, ob, vc

Fables	Elkan-Vogel	STTB, bn, fl, 2ob, st qt

ALAIN, JEHAN (1911-1940)
    Messe Modale en Septuor   Doblinger   SA, fl, st qt

ALBERT, HEINRICH (1604-1651)
    Ausgewählte Arien   Concordia   1-2V, bc
    * orig 8 vol

    12 Duets   Bärenreiter   2V, bc

ALEMANY, SUSANA F. DE
    5 Villancicos Comentados   Ricordi   V, gtr, rec, perc

ALEXANDER, JOSEF (1907-   )
    Songs for Eve   General   S, eng hn, hp, vc, vn
    * cycle of 15 songs in 2 vol

ALGAZI, LEON (1890-1971)
    4 Mélodies judéo-espagnoles   Salabert   medV, (fl,vc) (pf)(hp)

AMATO, BRUNO (1936-   )
    Two Together   Seesaw   S, tuba

AMBROSI, ALEARCO
    Voices   Sonzogno   S, nar, bn, cem, cl, fl, ob, st qt, vib

AMES, WILLIAM (1901-   )
    Among the Gods   ACA   S, cl, st qt

AMLIN, MARTIN (1953-   )
    Black Riders (S. Crane)   Seesaw, 1977   A, hp, pf, vc, vib,

    Requiem   Seesaw   A, chim, glk, vib

AMON, JOHANNES ANDREAS (1763-1825)
    An den Tod   Simrock   S, fl, pf(gtr)

AMRAM, DAVID (1930-   )
    Three Songs for America (J.F.   Peters   B, (bn, cl/bcl, fl,
       Kennedy, M.L. King, Jr., R.F.   hn, ob/eng hn,
       Kennedy)   st qnt)(pf)
    * 8'30"

ANDERS, ERICH (1883-   )
109   Flötenlieder   Zimmermann   S, fl, pf

ANDERSON, BETH (1950-   )
         Music for Myself   ACA   Ms, vib, visuals

         Paranoia   "   Ms, 2fl(pf)

         She Wrote (G. Stein, comp)   "   fV, tp, 2vn

         Tulip Cause   "   T, afl, bcl, cl,
                                                           db, org, timp, tp,
                                                           tsax, vc

ANDERSON, T.J. (1928-   )
         Beyond Silence (Hanson)   "   T, cl, pf, trbn,
         * 15'   va, vc

         Variations on a theme by M.B.   "   S, asax, pf, tpt,
           Tolson   trbn, vc, vn

ANDRIESSEN, HENDRIK (1892-1981)
         3 Romantic Songs   Donemus   Ms, fl, ob, pf

ANDRIESSEN, JURRIAAN (1925-   )
         Polderpastiches   "   Bar, cl, vc

ANTONIOU, THEODORE (1935-   )
         Chorochronos III   Bärenreiter, 1975 B, perc, pf, tp
           God (Bible)
           Time (T.S. Eliot)
           Cosmos (Bible)
           Sacred Book of Egypt (Orphic
             fragments, Brahman teaching)
           Death (Bible)
           Untitled (Pythagorean epigram
             on Temple of Delphi)
           Man; The Man (Bramanas and
             Upanishads)
           Being (Lao-Tzu)

         Epilogue: After the Odyssey by Bärenreiter, 1964 Ms, nar, db, gtr,
           Homer   hn, ob, perc, pf

         Moirologhia for Jani Christou: Bärenreiter, 1971 B, (cl, fl, gtr,
           Laments (Tolia)   2perc, pf)(pf)

ANTUNES, JORGE (1942-   )
         Microformobiles II   Zerboni   B, 5inst

APONTE-LEDEE, RAFAEL (1938-   )
    La Ventana Abierta   Seesaw, 1968   AAA, cel, cl, db,
                                                    3fl, hn, 2perc, pf,
                                                    tpt, vc, vn

APOSTEL, HANS ERICH (1901-1972)
22   5 Lieder (R. Felmayr)   Universal   medV, bn, cl, fl

ARANAZ, PEDRO (1742-1821)
    La Maja limonera   UME, 1970   ST, pf

ARENSKY, ANTON STEPANOVICH (1861-1906)
29   1 Minuti schastya (Apuktin)   Muzyka, 1967   SA, pf
      3 Fialka (Heine)

45   1 Tikho vsyo sred charuyushchey   "   SA, pf
        nochi (Seversky)
      2 Dve rozï (Plesheheyev)

55   2 Oni lyubili drug druga   "   SATB
        (Lermontov)

57   1 Serenada (Fet)   "   SATB, vc
      2 Ugasshim zvezdam (Fet)

ARGENTO, DOMINICK (1927-   )
    To Be Sung Upon the Water   Boosey, 1934   hiV, cl/bcl, pf
      (Wordsworth)
      1 Prologue
      2 The Lake at Evening
      3 Music on the Water
      4 Fair is the Swan
      5 In Remembrance of Schubert
      6 Hymn Near the Rapids
      7 The Lake at Night
      8 Epilogue: De Profundis

ARIOSTI, ATTILIO (1666-1729)
    L'Olmo   Deutscher   hiV, bc, 2vn

    La Rosa (It/Ger)   "   hiV, bc, 2vn

    Vuol ch'io parta   Carisch   S, bn, cl, fl, hp,
                                                      ob

ARNE, THOMAS (1710-1778)
    Nine Shakespeare Songs   Chappell, 1964
      Under the Greenwood Tree   V, kbd, pic(rec),
                                                      2vn
      Blow, blow, thou Winter Wind   V, kbd, 2vn(rec)
      The Cuckoo Song   V, kbd, fl(rec), 2vn
      The Owl   V, fl(rec), kbd, 2vn
      Come Away, Death   V, kbd, 2vn

Tell me where is Fancy bred?		V, kbd, 2vn
Come unto these yellow sands		V, kbd, vn(rec)
Ariel's Song		V, fl(vn), kbd, vn
Dirge in Cymbeline		V, kbd, 2vn
Tho' gaily the flowers: an appeal to Flora	Augener, 1934	SA(TB), pf

ARRIGO, GIROLAMO (1930-   )
    Quattro Episodi (Greek verse)   Heugel   S, fl

ASCONE, VICENTE (1897-1979)
    Montes de mi Quequay   Southern Peer   medV, pf qnt

ASTON, PETER (1938-   )
    My Dancing Day   Novello   ST, cl, fl, st qt

ASTORGA, EMANUELE D' (1680-1757)
    Vo cercando   Peters, <u>AMBC</u>, vol 2   SS, bc

ATOR, JAMES (1938-   )
    Haikansana   Seesaw   A, asax, ob, vc

AUBERT, LOUIS (1720-c. 1783)
    L'Heure Captive (Dommange)   Durand   B, pf, vn

AVNI, TZVI (1927-   )
    Collage (Y. Amihai)   Boosey   med(hi)V, fl, perc, tp

AVSHALOMOV, JACOB (1919-   )
    Little Clay Cart (ancient Hindu)   ACA   V, ban(gtr), cl, fl, perc, vc, vn

    Two Old Birds (Hopkins)   "   S, cl, pf

BABBITT, MILTON (1916-   )
    A Solo Requiem (Shakespeare, Dryden, Hopkins, Meredith, Stramm)   Peters   S, 2pf

    Composition for Tenor and 6 Instruments (comp)   AMP, 1960   T, fl, hpd, ob, st tr

    Philomel (J. Hollander)
    * 20'   AMP   S, tp

    Phonemena
    * 4'30"   Peters   S, tp(pf)

Two Sonnets (Hopkins)   Peters   Bar, cl, va, vc
* 7'30"

Vision and Prayer (Thomas)   AMP   S, syn
* 15'

BACH, CARL PHILIPP EMANUEL (1714-1788)
H   Phillis und Thirsis   Arno, 1972   SS, bc, 2fl
697

BACH, HEINRICH (1615-1692)
Ach, das Ich Wassers genug   Hänssler   A, bc, 3va, vc, vn
hatte

BACH, JOHANN CHRISTIAN (1735-1782)
4   Six canzonets   Breitkopf, 1958   SS, bc
1 Già la notte s'avicina
2 Ah rammenta o bella Irene
3 Pur nel sonno almen talora
4 T'intendo si mio cor
5 Che ciascun per te sospiri
6 Ascoltami, o Clori

6   Six Italian Duets   "   SS, bc
1 Torna in quel l'onda
2 Io lo so che il sembiante
3 E pur fra le tempeste
4 Trova un sol mia bella Clori
6 S'infida tu mi chiami

Four Scotch Songs   Schott, 1969
1 The Braes of Ballenden   A, ob, pf, va, vc,
   (T. Blacklock)   vn
2 I'll never leave thee   A, 2fl, pf, 2vn
   (R. Crawford)
3 Lochaber (A. Ramsey)   A, 2fl, pf, va, 2vn
4 The Broom of Cowdenknows   A, 2fl, pf, va, 2vn
* arr

BACH, JOHANN CHRISTOPH (1642-1703)
Wie bist du denn, O Gott   Hänssler, 1976   B, bc, 2va, vn
* 12'

BACH, JOHANN SEBASTIAN (1685-1750)
BWV   Quodlibit   Breitkopf, 1932   SATB, bc
524   * final fugue missing

BACH, WILHELM FRIEDEMANN (1710-1784)
Zerbrecht, zerreiszt, in   Leuckart   S, hn, org
schönen Bande

BACHELET, ALFRED (1864-1944)
    Chère Nuit   Leduc   S, pf, vn

BALFE, MICHAEL (1808-1870)
    Excelsior! (Longfellow)   Viking, 1973,   TB, pf
                                     The Parlor Song
                                     Book

BANCQUART, ALAIN (1934-   )
    Proche   Jobert   B, vc(va)

BANTOCK, SIR GRANVILLE (1868-1946)
    Three Songs from Greek   Swan   S, fl
        Anthology

BARAB, SEYMOUR (1921-   )
    Bagatelles   Galaxy   hiV, gtr, rec
    1 Prelude
    2 Roundelay (Dryden)
    3 Prue (T. Moore)
    4 The Fly (W. Blake)
    5 If Love Were What the Rose Is
      (Swinburne)
    6 Tom
    7 The Owl (Tennyson)
    8 The Pigtail (Thackeray)

BARBE, HELMUT (1927-   )
    Requiem 1965   Hänssler   S, bn, db, fl, ob,
                                             va, vc

BARBER, SAMUEL (1910-   )
  3   Dover Beach (Arnold)   G Schirmer   Bar(Ms), st qt

BARRAQUE, JEAN (1928-1973)
    Chant après chant (Barraque, Bruzzichelli   S, 6perc, pf
      Broch)

    Sequence (Nietzsche)   "   S, hp, 3perc, pf,
                                             vc, vib/cel/glk, vn

BASSETT, LESLIE (1923-   )
    Time and Beyond (Emerson,   Peters   Bar, cl, pf, vc
      Vanoren, Gitanjali, Tagore)
      * 9'

BAUMANN, MAX (1917-   )
    Die schöne Seilerin   Sirius   Ms, cl, db, fl, vn

BAUSSNERN, WALDEMAR VON (1866-1931)
    8 Kammergesänge   Schott, 1927   S, cl, fl, st qt

BAUTISTA, JULIAN (1901-1961)
    4 Cantos Callegos   Southern Peer   A, cl, fl, hp, ob,
                                                              va, vc

BAVICCHI, JOHN (1922-   )
        To the Lighthouse (Norma   Seesaw, 1971   S, hn, pf
        Farber)

        Trio No. 3   Seesaw   A, vc, vn

BAX, SIR ARNOLD (1883-1953)
    I heard a piper piping   Chappell   S, fl, pf
        (Campbell)

BEALE, JAMES (1924-   )
  28   Proverbs   ACA   Bar, eng hn,
                                                        pf(vc), vib

  33   3 Songs   "   S, va, vn

  35   Lamentations   "   S, fl, pf

BECKER, GUNTHER (1924-   )
    Fragments from "Hymnen an die G Schirmer   CtTBbar
        Nacht" (Novalis)

    Moirologi (H. Ilias)   Zimmermann   hiS, bcl, 2cl, hp

    Rigolo   Gerig   hiV, cl, fl, pf,
                                                        treb inst, vc, vn

BEDFORD, DAVID (1937-   )
    That White and Radiant Legend Universal   S, nar, 8inst
        (A.C. Clarke)
    * 14'30"

    The Tentacles of the Dark   Universal, 1975   T, db, 2va, 2vc, 3vn
        Nebula
    * 17'30"

    Music for Albion Moonlight   Universal, 1966   S, cl, fl, harm
                                                        with kbd, pf, vc, vn

BEDFORD, HERBERT (1867-1945)
    Night Piece No. 2 (The   Stainer, 1925   V, fl, ob, pf
        Shepherd)

BEEKHUIS, HANNA (1889-   )

3 Church Lieder	Donemus	V, pf, vc
Les Deux Flûtes	"	Ms, 2fl, pf
Dormeuse	"	3fV, fl, hp, vc
3 Lieder from Gazelle	"	S, pf, vc
Nocturne	"	SABar, pf
Reflêts du Japon	"	A, va

BEESON, JACK (1921-   )

A Creole Mystery (Hearn)	Boosey	medV, st qt
The Day's No Rounder than its Angles are (Viereck)	"	medV, st qt

BEETHOVEN, LUDWIG VAN (1770-1827)

82	Lebens-Genuss (Metastasio)	Peters, <u>Four Ariettas and a Duet</u>	ST, pf
100	Merkenstein (Rupprecht)	GA, xxiii	SA(TB), pf
118	Elegischer Gesang	Kalmus	SATB, st qt
	175 folksong arrangements * some available from Kalmus, Bärenreiter, Breitkopf, and Peters	GA, xxiv, HS xiv	1-4V, st tr

BENEDICT, SIR JULIUS (1804-1885)

The Bird that Comes	Ashdown	V, fl, pf
The Gypsy and the Bird	Boosey	V, fl, pf
The Wren (La Capinera)	Schirmer, 1881	S, fl, pf

BENGUEREL, XAVIER (1931-   )

Ballade von der singenden Frau in der Nacht	Bärenreiter, 1965	SSA, 7inst
Paraules de cada dia (Port/Ger)	Modern	Ms, cel, 2cl, 3fl, hp, pf, vib

BENHAMOU, MAURICE (1929-   )

Mizmor-chir (Heb-trans-literated)	Jobert, 1967	S, fl, hn, st qt, tpt, trbn, vib

BENJAMIN, ARTHUR (1893-1960)

The piper	Elkan-Vogel	S, fl, pf

BENNETT, RICHARD RODNEY (1936-   )
    Crazy Jane (Yeats)   Universal   S, cl, pf, vc

    Jazz Pastoral (Herrick)   "   V, db, hn, perc,
                                                        pf, 2sax, 2tpt,
                                                        trbn, tuba

    Tom O'Bedlam's Song   Belwin   T, vc

BENTON, DANIEL (1945-   )
    Dirge: In memoriam Igor   Seesaw   S, afl, bn, btrbn,
      Stravinsky   fl, 4perc, vc, vn

    Love Song   "   S(A), fl, hp

    Lux Aeterna   "   A, db, org

    2 Shakespeare Songs   "   S, bcl, fl, vn

BENVENUTI, ARRIGO (1925-   )
    Cantus Gemellus   Bruzzichelli   V, fl

BERGER, ARTHUR (1912-   )
    3 Poems of Yeats   New Mus Ed, 1950   V, cl, fl, vc
      Crazy Jane on the Day of
        Judgement
      His Confidence
      Girl's Song

BERGER, JEAN (1909-   )
    3 Canciones   Sheppard   V, fl, va, vc

    6 Rondeaux   "   V, va

    5 Songs (Mary Stuart)   "   medV, fl, va, vc

    4 Sonnets (Camoens) (Port/Eng)   G Schirmer   V, st qt(pf)

BERGMAN, WALTER (1902-   )
    Pastoral   Schott   A, fl

BERIO, LUCIANO (1925-   )
    Agnus   Universal, 1976   2fV, 3cl, drone

    Air   Universal   S, pf, va, vc, vn

    Chamber Music (Joyce)   Zerboni, 1954   V, cl, hp, vc

    Circles (cummings)   Universal, 1961   fV, hp, 2perc

    Cries (Cries of London)   Universal, 1976   6V(8V)

	El mar la mar (Alberti) * 1969 version	Universal, 1971	SS, acc, 2cl, db, fl, hp
	0 King	Universal, 1970	Ms, cl, fl, pf, vc, vn

	Folk Song arrangements
	  A la femminisca
	  Azerbaijan love song
	  Ballo
	  Black is the colour
	  I wonder as I wander
	  La donna ideale
	  Lo fiolaire
	  Loosin yelav
	  Malurous qu'o uno fenno
	  Mottettu
	  Rossignolet du bois
		Universal, 1968	Ms, cl, fl(pic),
			hp, pf, va, vc

BERLINSKI, HERMAN (1910-   )

		Psalm 23	Mercury, 1962	hiV, fl

BERLIOZ, HECTOR (1803-1869)

2	2	Hélène (Gounet, after Moore)	NBE, xv	SS(TB), pf
12		La Captive. Orientale (Hugo)	"	Ms, pf, vc
13	3	Le Trébuchet (Bertin, Deschamps)	"	SS(TB), pf
	4	Le jeune pâtre breton (Brizeux)	Breitkopf	S(T), hn, pf
18		Nocturne	NBE, xv	SS, gtr
		Amitié, reprends ton empire (Florian)	"	SSB, pf
		Aubade (Musset)	"	V, 2hn
		Le montagnard exilé (Duboys)	"	SS, hp(pf)
		Pleure, pauvre, Colette	"	SS(TT), pf

BERNHARD, CHRISTOPH (1628-1692)

		Aus der Tiefen ruf Ich, Herr, zu dir	Bärenreiter	S, bc, 2vn
		Fürchtet euch nicht *Christmas	"	S, bc, ob(vn), 2vn
		Jauchzet dem Herren	"	S, bc, 2vn
		Was betrübst du dich, meine Seele	"	A, bc, va, vc, vn

BERNIER, NICOLAS (1665–1734)
    Le Café   Bärenreiter, 1959   S, bc, vn(fl)
    * cantata

BEURLE, JURGEN (1943–   )
    Sinus (no text)   Moeck, 1959   SBar, perc, va, vn
    * 10'

BEYDTS, LOUIS (1895–1953)
    3 Mélodies   Durand   T, fl, pf

BEYER, JOHANN SAMUEL (1669–1744)
    Heilig ist Gott   Hänssler   ST, bc, 2rec

BEYER, JOHANNA (1888–1944)
    Ballad of the Star Eater   AMC   S, cl

    Have Faith   "   S, fl

    3 Songs   "   S, cl

    Stars, Songs, Faces   "   S, perc, pf

BHATIA, VANRAJ
    The Toy-Seller   Oxford   S, pf, vn

BIALAS, GUNTHER (1907–   )
    Gesang von den Tieren   Möseler   A, cl, fl, hpd, 2
                                             side drums, xyl

BIALOSKY, MARSHALL (1923–   )
    A Christmas Hymn   Seesaw   A, cl, fing cym,
                                             va, vc

    6 Riddles   "   med-hiV, trbn (bn),
                                             vc

    2 Songs   "   S, btrbn

    3 Songs   "   S, cl

    2 Voices in a Meadow   "   2medV, va

BIBER, HEINRICH VON (1644–1704)
    Nisi Dominus Aedificaverit Deutscher   B, vc, vn

BINKERD, GORDON (1916–   )
    Portrait Intérieur (Rilke) Boosey   Ms, vc, vn

    Secret Love (Dryden)   "   med-hiV, hp, vc

| | Three Songs (Crapsey, Herrick) | Boosey | Ms, st qt(pf) |

BIRTWHISTLE, HARRISON (1934-   )

	Cantata (Sappho, Greek Anthol.)	Universal	S, cl, fl, glk, vn(va), pic, pf(cel)
	Entr'actes and Sappho Fragments	Universal, 1965	S, fl, hp, ob, perc, va, vn
	Epilogue: Full Fathom Five (Shakespeare)	Universal	Bar, hn, 2perc, 4trbn
	Monody for Corpus Christi	Universal, 1965	S, fl, hn, vn
	Nenia on the Death of Orpheus (Zinovieff)	Universal	S, cl/bcl, crot, pf
	Prologue (Aeschulus)	Universal, 1979	T, bn, hn, 2tpt, trbn, vc, vn
	Ring a dumb Carillon (Logue)	Universal	S, cl, perc

BISHOP, SIR HENRY (1786-1855)

| | Four Songs | Curwen | V, fl, pf |
| | Lo! Here the Gentle Lark (Shakespeare) | G Schirmer | S, fl, pf |

BISSELL, KEITH (1912-   )

| | Overheard on a Salt Marsh | Kerby | Ms, fl, pf |
| | 4 Songs | Waterloo | S(T), hp |

BIZET, GEORGES (1838-1875)

| | La fuite (T. Gautier) | LC | ST, pf |

BJELINSKI, BRUNO (1909-   )

| | Candomble | Breitkopf | S, perc, pf |

BLACHER, BORIS (1903-1975)

1	Jazz Koloraturen * vocalise	Bote, 1929	S, asax, bn
47	Francesca da Rimini (Dante) (Ger)	Bote	S, vn
	5 Negro Spirituals (Eng/Ger) 1 Talk about a child that do love Jesus 2 My soul's been anchored in de Lord 3 Jesus walked this lonesome valley	Bote, 1962	Ms(Bar), 3cl, db, perc, trbn

4 Oh nobody knows the troubles
   I've seen
5 My good Lord done been here

Drei Psalmen	Bote	Bar, bn, cl, org, va, vc, vn
13 Ways of Looking at a Blackbird	"	hiV, st qt

BLANK, ALLAN (1925-   )

Being	ACA	S, cl
Coalitions	AMC	S, 2cl, perc, pf, trbn
Don't Let That Horse Eat That Violin	Seesaw	S, bn, opt vn
4 Dream Poems	AMC	S, cl, pf, tpt
Esther's Monologue	ACA	S, ob, va, vc
The Penny Candystore behind the El	Seesaw	S, bn
4 Poems (Dickinson)	ACA	S, cl, fl

BLISS, SIR ARTHUR (1891-1975)

10	Madame Noy (E.H.W. Meyerstein)	Chester, 1921	S, bn, cl, db, fl, hp, va
20	Two Nursery Rhymes (F. Cornford) 1 The Ragwort 2 The Dandelion	Chester, 1949	S, cl(va), pf
81	Elegiac Sonnet	Novello	T, pf, st qt
	Rhapsody	Stainer	ST, db, eng hn, fl, st qt

BLOW, JOHN (1649-1708)

Amphion Anglicus (facsimile)	Gregg, 1965	1-4V, bc
Chloe found Amintas (d'Urfey)		2V, bc
Come fill the Glass		2V, bc
Employed all the day long on public affairs		2V, bc
Go, purjur'd Man (Herrick)		2V, bc
Go, purjur'd maid		2V, bc
If I my Celia could persuade (G. Etherage)		2V, bc
Lately on yonder swelling bush (Waller)		2V, bc
Make bright your warrior's shield		2V, bc

Morpheus, the humble God (J. Denham)		2V, bc
Orethea's bright eyes		2V, bc
Prithee die, and set me free (Denham)		2V, bc
Shepherds, deck your crooks		3V, bc
Sing, sing ye muses		4V, bc
To me you made a thousand vows		2V, bc
When I drink my heart is possess't (Sir R. Howard)		2V, bc
When artists hit on lucky thoughts		2V, bc
Whence, Galatea, why so gay?		2V, bc
Whilst on Septimnius's panting breast (Cowley)		2V, bc
Whilst on your neck no rival boy		2V, bc
Why is Terpander pensive grown?		2V, bc
Ode on the Death of Mr. Henry Purcell	AMP	2Ct(2A), bc, 2rec

BLUMENFELD, HAROLD (1923-   )

Eroscapes (Isabella Gardner)	Seesaw	colS, st tr, ww qnt
La Vie Antérieure (after Baudelaire)	"	ATB, cbn, gtr, 5perc, pf, tp, 2va, 2vc
Voyages (after Hart Crane)	AMC	Bar, gtr, 2perc, va

BLUMER, THEODOR (1881-1964)

Das Deutsche Volkslied * Liederspiel	Sikorski	SB, fl, pf, va

BLYTON, CAREY (1932-   )

Symphony in Yellow (O. Wilde)	Boosey	hiV, hp

BOATWRIGHT, HOWARD (1918-   )

Black is the Color	Oxford	S, vn
Cock Robin	"	medV, rec(mel inst)
2 Folk Songs	"	S, vn
Gypsie Laddie	"	medV, 2mel inst
One Morning in May	"	medV, vn

BOESMANS, PHILIPPE (1936-   )
    Upon La-Mi   Jobert   S, amp hn, cl, db,
                                                                 fl, hp, perc, pf,
                                                                 vc, 2vn

BOIS, ROB DU (1934-   )
    Inferno   Donemus   S, hpd, vc, 2vn

        Pour faire chanter la Polonaise   "   S, fl, 3pf

        Songs of Innocence   "   TCt, db, rec

        Words   "   Ms, fl, pf, vc

BOND, VICTORIA (1950-   )
    Cornography   Seesaw   S, bn, hn

        Suite aux Troubadours   "   S, fl, lute, ob,
                                                                 va, vc

BONDON, JACQUES (1927-   )
    Le Pain de Serpent   Transat   S, bn, cl, fl,
                                                                 3perc, vc, vib, xyl

BONNER, EUGENE (1889-   )
    Flûtes   Chester, 1923   medV, bn, cl, fl,
                                                                 hp(pf), vc

BONONCINI, GIOVANNI (1670-1747)
8   Ten Duetti da camera   Peters   2V, bc

BORNEFELD, HELMUT (1906-   )
    Der Herr ist mein getreuer Hirt Bärenreiter   S, fl(rec), org

        Wie schonleuchtet der   Hänssler   SS, bc, fl, org,
          Morgenstern   va, vn

BORRIS, SIGFRIED (1906-   )
    3 Poems for Tenor   Sirius   T, bn, fl, hn, ob

BORTOLOTTI, MAURO (1926-   )
    Tre Poesie di Paul Eluard   Edi-Pan   S, cl, vc

BORTZ, DANIEL (1943-   )
    Melismer   Stim   S, hn

BORUP-JORGENSON, AXEL (1924-   )
55   Winterelegie   Fog   SMsA, bn, fl, ob,
                                                                 pf, va, vn

BOTTO, CARLOS (1923-   )
        Cantos al Amor y a la Muerte   Southern Peer   hiV, st qt
        (Sp/Eng)

BOULANGER, LILI (1893-1918)
        Renouveau (Silvestre)   Ricordi (LC)   SATB, pf
        * 8'

BOULEZ, PIERRE (1925-   )
        2 Improvizations sur Mallarmé   Universal   S, bells, hp,
                                                               4perc, vib

        Le Marteau sans Maître   "   A, fl, gtr, mar,
                                                               perc, va, vib

BOURDEAUX, LUC (1929-   )
        Canciones   Heugel   A, bn, cl, fl, hn,
                                                               ob

BOURLAND, ROGER (1952-   )
        Dickinson Madrigals   EC Schirmer   SMsTB

BOUVARD, FRANCOIS (1683-1760)
        Le temple de Baccus   Ear Mus Fac   Bar, bc, fl, vn

BOWLES, PAUL (1910-   )
        A Picnic Cantata (J. Schuyler)   LC   4fV, perc, 2pf

        Scènes d'Anabase (Perse)   "   T, ob, pf

BOXBERG, CHRISTIAN (1670-1729)
        Mache die Tore Weit   Hänssler   S, bc, 2rec, 2vn

BOZAY, ATTILA (1939-   )
        Papierschnitzel (M. Radnoti)   Boosey   S, cl, vc
        (orig in Hung)

BRAGA, GAETANO, (1829-1907)
        La Serenata   Bruzzichelli   S(T), pf,
        * also avail in low key   vn(vc)(mand)

BRAHMS, JOHANNES (1833-1897)
  20   Three Duets   Peters, Simrock   SA, pf
        1 Weg der Liebe, i
        2 Weg der Liebe, ii
        3 Die Meere

28	Four Duets	Peters	AB, pf

  1 Die Nonne und der Ritter
     (Eichendorff)
  2 Vor der Tür
  3 Es rauschet das Wasser (Goethe)
  4 Der Jäger und sein Liebchen
     (von Fallersleben)

31	Three Quartets	"	SATB, pf

  1 Wechsellied zum Tanz (Goethe)
  2 Neckereien
  3 Der Gang zum Liebchen

52	Liebeslieder (G.F. Daumer)	Peters, Schott	SATB, pf 4 hnds

  1 Rede, Mädchen, allzu liebes   unless otherwise
  2 Am Gesteine rauscht die Flut   indicated
  3 O die Frauen   TB, pf 4hnds
  4 Wie des Abends schöne Rote   SA, pf 4hnds
  5 Die grüne Hopfenranke
  6 Ein kleiner, hübscher Vogel
  7 Wohn schon bewandt war es   S(A), pf 4hnds
  8 Wenn so lind dein Auge mir
  9 Am Donaustrande
  10 O wie sanft die Quelle
  11 Nein, es ist nicht auszukommen
  12 Schlosser auf, und mache
     Schlosser
  13 Vögelein durchrauscht die Luft   SA, pf 4hnds
  14 Sieh, wie ist die Welle klar   TB, pf 4hnds
  15 Nachtigall, sie singt so schön
  16 Ein dunkeler Schacht ist Liebe
  17 Nicht wandle, mein Licht   T, pf 4hnds
  18 Es bebet das Gestrauche

61	Four Duets	Peters, Simrock	SA, pf

  1 Die Schwestern (Mörike)
  2 Klosterfräulein (Kerner)
  3 Phänomen (Goethe)
  4 Die Boten der Liebe

64	Three Quartets	Peters	SATB, pf

  1 An die Heimat (Sternau)
  2 Der Abend (Schiller)
  3 Fragen (Daumer)

65	Neue Liebeslieder (Daumer)	Peters	SATB, pf 4hnds

  1 Verzicht, o Herz, auf Rettung   unless otherwise
  2 Finstere Schatten der Nacht   indicated
  3 An jeder Hand die Finger
  4 Ihr Schwarzen Augen
  5 Wahre, wahre, deine Sohn
  6 Rosen steckt mir an die Mutter   S, pf 4hnds
  7 Vom gebirge Well' auf Well'
  8 Weiche Graser im Revier
  9 Nagen am Herzen   S, pf 4hnds
  10 Ich Kose suss mit der und der   T, pf 4hnds
  11 Alles, alles in den Wind   S, pf 4hnds
  12 Schwarzer Wald, dein Schatten
  13 Nein, Geliebter, setze dich   SA, pf 4hnds

	14 Flammenauge, dunkles Haar		
	15 Zum Schluss		
66	Five Duets	Peters, Simrock	SA, pf
	1 Klänge, i (Groth)		
	2 Klänge, ii		
	3 Am Strande (Hölty)		
	4 Jägerlied (Candidus)		
	5 Hüt du dich!		
75	Four Ballads and Romances	Peters	
	1 Edward		AT, pf
	2 Guter Rat		SA, pf
	3 So lass un wandern!		ST, pf
	4 Walpurgisnacht (W. Alexis)		SS, pf
91	Two Songs	Peters, Simrock, International	A, pf, va
	1 Gestillte Sehnsucht (Rückert)		
	2 Geistliches Wiegenlied (Geibel)		
92	Four Quartets	Peters	SATB, pf
	1 O schöne Nacht (Daumer)		
	2 Späterbst (H. Allmers)		
	3 Abendlied (F. Hebbel)		
	4 Warum? (Goethe)		
103	Zigeunerlieder (trad. Hung)	"	SATB, pf
	1 He, Zigeuner, greife		
	2 Hochgetürmte, Rimaflut		
	3 Wisst ihr, wann mein Kindchen		
	4 Lieber Gott, du weisst		
	5 Brauner Bursche führt zum Tanze		
	6 Röslein dreie in der Reihe		
	7 Kommt dir manchmal		
	8 Horch, der Wind klagt		
	9 Weit und breit schaut niemand		
	10 Mond verhüllt sein Angesicht		
	11 Rote Abendwolken ziehn		
112	Six Quartets	"	SATB, pf
	1 Sehnsucht (Kugler)		
	2 Nächtens (Kugler)		
	3 Vier Zigeunerlieder, no. 1		
	4 Vier Zigeunerlieder, no. 2		
	5 Vier Zigeunerlieder, no. 3		
	6 Vier Zigeunerlieder, no. 4		
	Kleine Hochzeitkantate (G. Keller)	BW, xx	SATB, pf

BRAND, MAX (1896-1980)

	5 Songs	Universal	S, cl, fl, hn, ob, vc, vn

BRANDT BUYS, JAN (1868-1939)

20	3 Lieder	Dreiklang	V, fl, pf

BRANDT, FRITZ
  29   4 Lieder   Kultura   V, fl, pf

BRANT, HENRY (1913-   )
         Admonition   ACA   A, chim, pf, 3trbn
         * 7'

BRESGEN, CESAR (1913-   )
         4 Songs after Afro-American   Breitkopf   S, perc, pf
         clack lyrics

BRITTEN, BENJAMIN (1913-1976)
  27   Hymn to St. Cecilia (Auden)   Boosey, 1937   SSATB

  51   Canticle II: Abraham and Isaac   Boosey, 1953   AT, pf
         * 17'

  55   Canticle III: Still Falls the   Boosey, 1956   T, hn, pf
         Rain-the Raids (Sitwell)

         Canticle IV: Journey of the   Faber, 1972   CtTBar, pf
         Magi

  89   Canticle V: The Death of Saint   Faber, 1976   T, hp
         Narcissus (Eliot)
         * 7'

  92   A Birthday Hansel (Burns)   Faber, G Schirmer,   hiV, hp
         * 16' 30"   1978

         Two Ballads   Boosey, 1937   2V, pf
         1 Mother Comfort (M. Slater)
         2 Underneath the Abject Willow
           (W.H. Auden)

BRUCKNER, ANTON (1824-1896)
         Ave Maria   Leuckart   A, st qt

BRUGK, HANS MELCHIOR (1909-   )
  18   Leuchtende Nacht (Carossa)   Benjamin, 1966   medV, fl, pf

BRUHNS, NICOLAUS (1665-1697)
         De Profundis Clamavi   Peters   B, org, vc, 2vn

         Der Herr hat seinen Stuhl im   "   B, bn, org, 2va,
           Himmel bereitet   vc, 2vn

         Erstanden ist der heilige   "   TT(SS), org, vc, 2vn
           Christ

         Hemmt eure Tränenflut   "   SATB, bn, org, 2va,
                                                                    vc, 2vn

Jauchzet dem Herren alle Welt	Peters	T(S), org, vc, 2vn
Mein Herz ist bereit	"	B, org, vc, vn

BURKHARD, WILLY (1900-1955)
36   Herbst (Morgenstern)   Schott   S, pf, vc, vn

BUSSOTTI, SYLVANO (1931-   )
     Siciliano   Bruzzichelli   12mV

BUXTEHUDE, DIETRICH (1637-1707)

Title	Publisher	Scoring
Afferte Domino gloriam honorem	G, v	SSB, bc
Alles was ihr tut	S, 39	SATB, bc, 5st
Also hat Gott die Welt geliebet	Chester, 1980	S, bc, gam, 2vn
An filius non est Dei	G, vii	ATB, bc, 3gam(3trbn)
Aperite mihi portas justitiae	Peters, 1953	ATB, bc, 2vn
Bedenke, Mensch, das Ende	G, v	SSB, bc, 3vn, vle
Befiehl dem Engel, dass er komm	G, viii	SATB, bc, vle, 2vn
Canite Jesu nostro	Bärenreiter, 1974	SSB, bc, vle, 2vn
Cantate Domino canticum novum	Bärenreiter, 1953	SSB, bc
Das neugeborne Kindelein	G, viii	SATB, bc, vle, 3vn
Der Herr is mit mir	"	SATB, bc, vle, 2vn
Dixit Dominus Domino meo	G, ii	S(T), bc, 2va, 2vn
Drei schöne Dinge sind	G, iii	SB, bc, vle, 2vn
Du Frieden-Fürst, Herr Jesu Christ	G, v	SSB, bc, bn, 4st
Ecce nunc benedicite Domino	G, viii	ATTB, bc, va, 2vn
Eins bitte ich vom Herrn	S, 15	SSATB, bc, 5st
Entreisst euch, meine Sinnen	Merseburger, 1959	S, bc, vle, 2vn
Erhalt uns, Herr, bei deinem Wort	G, viii	SATB, bc, vle(bn), 2vn
Fried und Freudenreiche Hinfarth	G, ii	
1 Mit Fried und Freud		4V
2 Klagelied		S, bc, 2st
Fallax mundus, ernat vultus	G, i	S, bc, 2vn

Gen Himmel zu dem Vater mein	G, i	S, bc, gam, vn
Gott hilf mir	S, 57	SSATB, bc, 5st
Herr, auf dich traue ich	G, i	S, bc, 2vn
Herr, nun lässt du deinen Diener	"	T, bc, 2vn
Herr, wenn ich nur dich hab'	"	S, bc, 2vn
Herr, wenn ich nur dich habe	"	S, bc, vle, 2vn
Herren vär Gud	G, viii	SATB, bc, vle, 2vn
Ich bin eine Blume zu Saron	G, ii	B, bc, vle, 2vn
Ich habe Lust abzuscheiden	G, v	SSB, bc, vle(bn), 2vn
Ich halte es dafür	G, iii	SB, bc, va, vle, vn
Ich sprach in meinem Herzen	G, i	S, bc, bn, 3vn
Ich suchte des Nachts	G, iii	TB, bc, 2ob, vle, 2vn
In dulci jubilo	G, v	SSB, bc, 2vn
In te, Domine, speravi	G, vii	SAB, bc
Je höher du bist	G, v	SSB, bc, vle, 2vn
Jesu dulcis memoria	G, vii	SS, bc, vle, 2vn
Jesu dulcis memoria	G, iii	ATB, bc, 2vn
Jesu komm mein Trost und Lachen	G, vii	ATB, bc, 4st
Jesu meine Freud und Lust	G, ii	A, bc, 4st
Jesu meine Freude	G, v	SSB, bc, bn, 2vn
Jesulein, du Tausendschön	G, vii	ATB, bc, vle(bn), 2vn
Jubilate Domino, omnis terra	G, ii	A, bc, gam
Kommst du, Licht der Heiden	G, vi	SSB, bc, 5st
Lauda anima mea Dominum	G, i	S, bc, vle, 2vn
Lauda Sion Salvatorem	G, vi	SSB, bc, gam, 2vn
Laudate pueri Dominum	G, iii	SS, bc, vle, 5gam
Liebster, miene Seele saget	"	SS, bc, 2vn
Lobe den Herrn, meine Seele	G, ii	T, bc, 2va, 3vn

Mein Herz ist bereit	G, ii	B, bc, vle, 3vn
Meine Seele, willtu ruhn	G, vi	SSB, bc, vle, 2vn
Missa Brevis	G, iv	SSATB, bc
Nichts soll uns scheiden	G, vii	SAB, bc, vle, 2vn
Nun freut euch, ihr Frommen	G, iii	SS, bc, 2vn
Nun lasst uns Gott dem Herren	G, viii	SATB, bc, vle, 2vn
O clemens, o mitis	G, i	S, bc, 4st
O dulcis Jesu	"	S, bc, 2vn
O fröhliche Stunden	"	S, bc, vle 2vn
O Gottes Stadt	G, i	S, bc, va, vle, 2vn
O Jesu mi dulcissime	G, vi	SSB, bc, vle, 2vn
O lux beata trinitas	G, iii	SS, bc, bn, 3vn
O wie selig sind	"	AB, bc, vle, 2vn
Quemadmodum desiderat cervus	G, ii	T, bc, 2vn
Salve desiderium	G, vi	SSB, bc, vle(bn), 2vn
Salve, Jesu, Patris gnate unigenite	G, iii	SS, bc, 2vn
Schaffe in mir, Gott, ein rein Herz	G, i	S, bc, vle, 2vn
Sicut Moses exaltavit serpentem	"	S, bc, gam, 2vn
Singet dem Herrn ein neues Lied	G, i	S, bc, vn
Surrexit Christus hodie	G, vi	SSB, bc, bn, 3vn
Wachet auf	G, vii	ATB, bc, 2vn
Wachet auf, ruft uns die Stimme	G, vi	SSB, bc, bn, 4vn
Walts Gott mein Werk ich lasse	G, viii	SATB, bc, vle, 2vn
Wär Gott nicht mit uns diese Zeit	"	SATB, bc, 2vn
Was frag' ich nach der Welt	G, vii	SAB, bc, vle, 2vn
Was mich auf dieser Welt betrübt	G, i	S, bc, 2vn
Welte, packe dich	G, vi	SSB, bc, vle, 2vn

Wenn ich, Herr Jesu, habe dich	G, ii	A, bc, 2vn
Wie schmeckt es so lieblich	G, vii	SAB, bc, vle, 2vn
Wie soll ich dich empfangen	G, vi	SSB, bc, bn, 2vn
Wo ist doch mein Freund gelieben	G, iii	SB, bc, bn, 2vn
Wo soll ich fliehen hin	S, 85	SATB, bc, 5st

CACCINI, FRANCESCA (1587-c. 1640)

Arie für Sopran	FMA	S, bc, 2fl(2vn)
O che nuovo stupore	Peters	Ms, bc, va(fl)(ob)(rec)

CACIOPPO, GEORGE (1927-   )

Time on time in Miracles	Berandol	S, btrbn, 2hn, perc, pf, ttrbn, vc

CAGE, JOHN (1912-   )

Forever and Sunsmell (e.e. cummings) * 5'	Peters	medV, 2perc

CALDARA, ANTONIO (1670-1736)

Haec est regina virginum	Bieler	S, bc, 2vn
8 Motetti	DTO, vol 26	2-3V, bc
Vaghe Luci	Peters, AMBC, vol 2	A, bc, vn

CALLAWAY, ANN (1949-   )

Besides This May (Dickinson)	AMC	S, fl, pf

CAMPRA, ANDRE (1660-1744)

Arion (Fr) * cantata	Heugel, 1974	S, bc, fl
Domine, Dominus noster * cantata	Bieler	S, bc, vn(fl)
l'hymen * cantata	Sikorski	V, bc, fl, vn

CANTELOUBE, JOSEPH (1879-1957)

A Bethléem, Quand l'Enfant Dieu * Christmas	Durand	SAT, pf

CAPDEVIELLE, PIERRE (1906-1969)
    Les amours de Ronsard   Ricordi   V, fl, hp, va, vc,
                                                          vn

CAPLET, ANDRE (1878-1925)
    Corbeille de fruits   Durand, 1924   V, fl

    Deux Sonnets   Durand   medV, hp
        Doux Fut le Trait
        Quand Reverrai-Je Hélas

    2 Mélodies   "   V, fl, pf

    Ecoute mon coeur (Tagore)   Durand, 1925   V, fl
    * 4'10"

    Viens! Une flûte invisible   "   V, fl, pf
        soupire
    * 2'5"

CAPRICORNUS, SAMUEL (1628-1665)
    Der gerechten Seelen sind in   Bärenreiter   SATB, bc, vc, 2vn
        Gottes Hand

    Mein Gott und Herr   "   SSB, bc, 2vn

CARILLO, JULIAN (1875-1965)
    Preludio a Colon (Version II)   Jobert   S, fl, gtr, hp, va,
                                                          vc, 2vn

CARISSIMI, GIACOMO (1605-1674)
    2 Cantatas   NYPL   1-3V, bc
    * 1 trio, 1 duet

    Chamber Duets: Peters, 1927   SS, bc(pf)
        A piu d'un verde alloro
        Ahi, non torna
        Il mio core e un mar di pianti
        Lungi omai
        Rimanti in pace
        Vaghi rai

    Jubilemus omnes et cantemus   Bärenreiter, 1973   SSB, bc
        (Lat/Ger)

    Summi regis puerpera   Oxford, 1982   SS, bc, 2vn

CARNICER, RAMON (1789-1855)
    El Musico y el Poeta   Bärenreiter, 1973   SSB, bc

CASANOVA, ANDRE (1919-   )
    Divertimento   Jobert   Ms, bn, cl, fl, ob,
                                                          pf, vc, vn

CASTLE, ZILLAH
    2 Miniatures   Schott   A(S), pf, treb rec

CEELEY, ROBERT (1930-   )
    Lullaby (C. Gascoigne)   ACA, 1979   S, trbn

CESTI, ANTONIO (1623-1669)
    Cantatas: A-R Ed, 1969
      Amante gigante   3V, bc
      Cara e dolce liberta, iii   2V, bc
      L'amoroso veleno, dialogo   2V, bc
      Lacrime mie   2V, bc
      Lasciate pu   2V, bc
      Misero cor   2V, bc
      Pria ch'adori   2V, bc
      Quante volte guirai   2V, bc
      Soffrite, tacete   2V, bc
      T'amo Filli   3V, bc

CHADWICK, GEORGE (1854-1931)
    Come Unto Me (Bartley)   G Schirmer   ST, pf

CHAMINADE, CECILE (1857-1944)
    L'Angelus (A. Silvestre)   Enoch   MsB, pf

    Portrait (P. Reynell)   "   T, fl, pf

CHAN, PIERRE
    La Jeune Parque (Valery)   Bomart   S, fl, hp, st tr

CHANCE, NANCY (1931-   )
    Darksong   Seesaw   S, 2cl, 2fl, gtr,
                                             hp, 2hn, 5perc, pf

    Duos 1   "   S, fl

    Edensong   "   S, cl, fl, hp,
                                               perc, vc, vib

    3 Poems by Rilke   "   S, eng hn, fl, vc

CHANLER, THEODORE (1902-1961)
    Portrait of a Matriarch   AMC   2hiV, fl, obb fl

CHARPENTIER, MARC-ANTOINE (c.1645-1704)
    Jesu Corona Virginum   Broekmans, 1971   SMs, bc, fl

CHAUSSON, ERNEST (1855-1899)
11   1 La Nuit (T. de Banville)   Hamelle, 1924,   2V, pf
                                  Vingt Mélodies

	2	Réveil (Balzac)	Leduc	
18	3	Duo de Junon et Cérès (Shakespeare)	HMA	ST, pf
37		Chanson Perpétualle	Durand	S(Ms), st qt(pf)
		Cantique de Sainte Cécile a la Vièrge Immaculée	Salabert	hiV, org, vc

CHERUBINI, LUIGI (1760-1842)

Four Duets Ahi, ch'e il suon del rio che frange Dite almeno, amiche fronde La mia Fille, il mio bel fuoco Solitario bosco ombroso	Peters, 1887	SS, pf
La Primavera	LC	SATB, pf

CHILDS, BARNEY (1926-   )

7 Epigrams	Tri-ten	S, cl

CHOU, WEN-CHUNG (1923-   )

7 Poems of the T'ang Dynasty	New Mus Ed, 1952	T, bn, cl, fl(pic), hn, ob, perc, pf, tpt, trbn

CIARDI, CESARE (1818-1877)

Le Rossignol	Kistner	S, fl, pf

CLARK, HENRY LELAND (1907-   )

4 Elements	ACA	S, vc
Emily Dickinson Canons	"	medV, va(vc)(vn)
Life in Ghana	"	medV, fl, pf
The Lord is My Shepherd	"	hiV, fl, timp(db)
Mercy, Pity, Peace and Love	"	SA, fl, ob, perc
The Quality of Mercy	"	SA, fl, ob, perc
Rondeau Redouble	"	Ms(Bar), bn, cl, vc
Song to a Young Pianist	"	medV, fl

CLEMENTI, ALDO (1925-   )

Silben	Zerboni	fV, cl, 2pf, vn

CLERAMBAULT, LOUIS-NICOLAS (1676-1749)
        Two cantatas: A-R Ed, 1979
        1 L'île de Delos   S, bc, bn, fl, ob,
                                                                  timp, tpt, vn
        2 La muse de l'opéra   S, bc, fl, vn

        Léandre et Héro   Rouart   V, bc, fl, va, vn
        * cantata

        Orphée   Faber, 1972   hiV, bc, fl, vn
        * cantata

COHEN, EDWARD (1940-   )
        3 Songs   Bomart   SMs, va, vc

        Serenade for a Summer Evening   "   SSATTB, cl, 2fl,
          (e.e. cummings)   va, vn

        The Ruin (Alexander)   "   S, pf, vn

CONSOLI, MARC ANTONIO (1941-   )
        3 Canzoni   ACA   S, fl, vc

        Equinox 1   "   Ms, fl, perc, pf, vc

        Equinox II   "   medV, cel, cl, fl,
                                                                  perc, pf, vc, vib,
                                                                  vn

        Isotonic   "   S, chim, fl, 2perc,
                                                                  pf, vib, xyl

CONSTANT, FRANZ (1910-   )
30   Triade   "   medV, asax, perc, pf

CONVERSE, FREDERICK (1871-1940)
        Spring Song (Virgil)   NEC   V, fl, pf

COOKE, ARNOLD (1906-   )
        Kaleidoscope   Seesaw   S, pf, slides, vc,
                                                                  vn

        Nocturnes   Oxford   S, hn, pf
          Boat Song (J. Davidson)
          Returning, we hear the larks
            (I. Rosenberg)
          River Roses (D.H. Lawrence)
          The Moon (Shelley)
          The Owl (Tennyson)
        * 5'

        Songs of Innocence (Blake)   Oxford, 1960   hiV, cl, pf

COPLAND, AARON (1900-   )
         As it fell upon a day   Boosey, 1956   S, cl, fl
            (R. Barnefield)

COPLEY, IAN (1926-   )
         In Babylon Town   Hinshaw   2medV, fl, opt snare

CORNELIUS, PETER (1824-1874)
   6   1 Liebesprobe (Hebbel)   H, ii   SB, pf
         2 Der beste Liebesbrief (Hebbel)
         3 Ein Wort der Liebe (Tegernsee)

  16   1 Heimatgedanken (A. Becker)   "   SB, pf
         2 Brennende Liebe (Mosen)
         3 Komm herbei, Tod (Shakespeare)
         4 Scheiden (H. von Fallersleben)

         Am Meer (Eichendorff)   "   SB, pf

         Ich und Du   "   SB, pf

         In Sternennacht (Heyse)   "   SS(ST), pf

         Irisch: O kennt ihr nicht   "   SA
            Emmchen (Comp)

         Irisch: Was trauern doch die   "   SA
            Mägdelein (comp)

         Mainzer Magdeleid (comp)   "   SB, pf

         Mein Liebchen ist nicht   "   SA
            Heliotrop (comp)

         Scheiden und Meiden (Ühland)   "   SS(ST), pf

         Verratene Liebe (Chamisso)   "   ST, pf

         Zu den Bergen hebet sich ein   "   SB, pf
            Augenpaar (Psalm 21)

CORTESE, LUIGI (1899-1976)
   8   Dues Canti Persiani   Zerboni   medV, fl, pf

  21   Salmo VIII   "   S, fl, pf, vc

COULTHARD, JEAN (1908-   )
         A Cradle Song   Berandol   SA, pf

COUPERIN, FRANCOIS (1668-1733)
         Audite omnes et expanescite   C, xii   Ct, bc, 2vn

Neuf Motets	Heugel, 1972, Le Pupitre	
Ad te Levavi oculos meos		B, bc, 2vn
Domine Salvum Fac Regem		SB, bc
Lauda Sion Salvatorem		SS, bc
Regina Coeli Laetare		SS, bc
Respice in me		Ct, bc
Salve Regina		Ct, bc
Salvum me fac Deus		B, bc
Tantum Ergo Sacramentum		SSB, bc
Usquequo, Domine		CT, bc
Quatre Versets d'un motet (Psalm cxviii)	C, xi	
Adolescentulus sum		S, 2fl, vn
Ignitum eloquium tuum		SS, bc, 2vn
Justitia tua		S, S, SS, bc
Qui dat nivem		S, 2fl, vn
Tabescere me		SS
Sept Versets (Psalm LXXIX)	"	
Deus virtutum convertere		Ct, bc, bviol, fl, ob
Dux itineris fuisti		B, bc, 2fl, 2ob, 2vn
Excita potentiam tuam		CtB, bc
Extendit palmites suos		S, bc, 2fl, vn
Operuit montes		S, bc, 2fl, vn
Qui regis Israel		CtTB, bc, 2vn
Vineam de Aegypto		B, bc, vn
Sept Versets d'un motet (Psalm LXXXIV)	"	
Audiam quid loquatur		B, bc, 2vn
Converte nos		B, bc, fl
Et enim Dominus		S, 2fl, 2ob
Misericordia et veritas		TT, bc
Numquid in aeternum		TBar, bc
Ostende nobis		CT, bc, fl(vn)
Veritas de terra		S, bc, vn
Trois Vestales Champêtres et Trois Policons	L'Oiseau	SSS, bc
Troisième Leçon de Ténèbres	"	SS(TT), bc
COWELL, HENRY (1897–1965)		
Toccanta	Boosey, 1960	S, fl, pf, vc
Tom Binkley's Tune	Merrymount	V, hn, pf
Vocalise * 8'	Peters, 1964	S, fl, pf
CRAS, JEAN (1879–1932)		
Fontaines	Senart	V, fl
La Flûte de Pan	Senart, 1930	V, fl, va, vc, vn

CRAWFORD, RUTH (1901–1953)
    3 Songs for Contralto   Merion   A, ob, perc, pf
      (Sandburg)
    1 Rat-Riddles
    2 Prayers of Steel
    3 In Tall Grass

CRUMB, GEORGE (1929–   )
    Ancient Voices of Children   Peters, 1970   SbS, elec pf, hn,
    * 25'   mand, ob, 3perc

    Lux Aeterna   Peters, 1971   S, bfl(treb rec),
    * 15'   perc, sitar

    Madrigals, Book I (Lorca)   Peters, 1965   S, db, vib
    * 9'

    Madrigals, Book II (Lorca)   "   S, fl/afl/pic, perc
    * 6'30"

    Madrigals, Book III (Lorca) Peters, 1969   S, hp, perc
    * 7'30"

    Madrigals, Book IV (Lorca)   "   S, db, fl/afl/pic,
    * 9'   hp, perc

    Night of the Four Moons (Lorca) "   A, afl/pic, ban,
    * 16'   elec vc, perc

    Night Music (Lorca)   Peters, 1963   S, 2perc, pf/cel

    Songs, Drones and Refrains of Peters   Bar, elec db, elec
      Death (Lorca)   gtr, elec pf/elec
    * 30'   hpd, 2perc

CUMMING, RICHARD (1928–   )
    As Dew in April   Boosey   medV, ob(cl)(vn)

DALLAPICCOLA, LUIGI (1904–1975)
    5 canti   Zerboni, 1956   B, afl, bcl, cl,
                                          fl, hp, pf, va, vc

    6 carmina Alcaei   Zerboni, 1943   S, bn, cl, fl, hp,
                                          ob, pf, tpt, trbn,
                                          va, vc, vn

    Divertimento in quattro   Zerboni, 1956   S, cl, fl/pic, ob,
      esercizi   va, vc

    Goethe lieder   Zerboni, 1953   S, 3cl

    2 liriche di Anacreonte   Zerboni, 1945   hiV, 2cl, pf, va

    Parole di San Paolo   Zerboni, 1964   Ms, afl, bcl, cel
                                          (pf), 2cl, hp, va,
                                          vc, vib, xyl

Sicut umbra   Zerboni, 1970   Ms, 12inst

DANIEL-LESUR (1908–   )
    4 Songs   Durand   hiV, fl, hp, va,
                                                    vc, vn

DANIELS, MABEL WHEELER (1878–1971)
    In a Manger Lowly   NEC   S, pf, vn

    Two Duets (O. Khayyam)   BPL, HL   SA, pf
    Love, the Fair Day
    O Love, How Green the World!

DANZI, FRANZ (1763–1826)
 16   Sechs dreistimme Gesange Breitkopf (LC)   SSB, pf

       Sei Quartetti   Simrock (LC)   SSTB, pf
       Del sen gl'ardori nessun mi
         vanti
       * 2'
       Se intende si poco che ho
         l'alma piagata
       * 2'30"
       Se per tutti ordisce amore
       *1'45"
       Se un core annodi se un alma
         accendi
       * 3'30"
       So che presto ognun s'avvede
       * 3'
       Sol puo dir come si trova
       * 2'15"

DARGOMIZHSKY, ALEXANDER (1813–1869)
       Vocal ensembles: C, 1950
       Chto mne do pesen   2V, pf
       Chto, moy svetik luna   2V, pf
         (Vyazemsky)
       Deva i roza (Delvig)   2V, pf
       Esli vstrechus's toboy   2V, pf
         (Koltsov)
       K druzyam (Pushkin)   2V, pf
       Kamen tyazholïy   2V, pf
       Minuvshikh dney ocharovanya   2V, pf
         (Delvig)
       Molitva   4V, pf
       Nad mogiloy (Delvig)   4V, pf
       Nenaglyadnaya tï   2V, pf
       Nochevala tuchka zolotaya   3V, pf
       Nocturne   2V, pf
       Rïtsari (Pushkin)   2V, pf
       Schastliv, kto ot khlada let   2V, pf
         (Zhukovsky)
       Skazhi, chto tak zadumchiv   3V, pf
         tï? (Zhukovsky)

Tï i vï (Pushkin)		2V, pf
Vladiko dney moikh (Pushkin)		2V, pf

DAUS, AVRAHAM (1902-1974)
| Songs of Rahel | Israeli, 1952 | A, fl, va |

DAVID FELICIEN (1810-1876)
| Charmant Oiseau | Schott | S, fl, pf |

DAVIES, PETER MAXWELL (1934-   )
Blind Man's Buff * 20'	Boosey, 1972	Ms, mime, cl, fl, gtr, perc, pf, vc, vn
Fiddlers at the Wedding (Mackay Brown) * 19'	Boosey, 1973	Ms, afl, gtr, mand, perc
Fools' Fanfare (Shakespeare) * 7'	Boosey, 1972	spkr, 2perc, 2trbn, 2tpt, uk/mand
From Stone to Thorn (Mackay Brown) * 20'	Boosey, 1971	Ms, bshn(acl), gtr, hpd, perc
Hymn to St. Magnus * 37'	Boosey, 1972	S, bshn, fl, perc, pf(hpd)(cel), va, vc
Leopardi Fragments	Schott	SA, hp, trbn, tpt, vc, ww qt
Miss Donnithorne's Maggot (Stow) * 32'	Boosey, 1974	Ms, cl, fl, perc, pf, vc, vn
Missa super l'homme armé * 20'	Boosey, 1968	V/spkr, cl, fl/pic, kbd, perc, vc, vn
Eight Songs for a Mad King (Stow and George III) * 33'	Boosey, 1969	mV, cl, fl/pic, kbds, perc, vc, vn
Tenebrae super Gesualdo * 20'	Boosey, 1972	Ms, cl, fl, gtr, hpd, perc, va, vc

DAVIES, SIR HENRY WALFORD (1869-1941)
| Songs of Nature | Curwen | SATB, st qt |

DEL TREDICI, DAVID (1937-   )
| I Hear An Army (Joyce) | Peters, 1964 | S, st qt |
| Night Conjure-verse (Joyce) | Boosey, 1965 | S(Ms)(Ct), bn, cl,
cl/bcl, fl, fl/pic,
hn, ob, va, vc, 2vn |

DELAGE, MAURICE (1879-1961)
    Alouette (du Bartas)   Durand, 1925   hiV, fl, pf

    4 poèmes hindous   Durand, 1913   S, bn, cl, fl, ob,
    1 Madras. Une Belle.   pf, st qt
    2 Lahores. Un sapin isole.
    3 Benares. Naissance de
        Bouddha.
    4 Jeypur. Si vous pensez.

DELANNOY, MARCEL (1898-1962)
    Deux Poèmes   Heugel   V, fl, pf, st qt

    Trois Histoires   "   V, bn, fl, pf

DELIBES, LEO (1836-1891)
    Le Rossignol (Eng/Fr/Ger)   Zimmermann   hiV, fl, pf

DELLO JOIO, NORMAN (1913-   )
    Lamentation of Saul   C Fischer, 1954   Bar, cl, fl, ob,
    * 20'   pf, va, vc

DESPORTES, YVONNE (1907-   )
    Polka (no text)   Eschig   SA, pf

DIAMOND, DAVID ((1915-   )
    The Mad Maid's Song   Southern Peer,   S, fl, hpd(pf)
    * 5'   1960

    Vocalises for Voice and Violin Southern Peer   S, va
    * 10'

DIDOMENICA, ROBERT (1927-   )
    Four Short Songs (Bobrowski)   Margun, 1976   S, cl, fl, pf, va,
                                             vc, vn

DIEMER, EMMA LOU (1927-   )
    4 Chinese Love Poems   Seesaw, 1976   S, hp(pf)

    3 Mystic Songs (Hindu poetry)   "   SBar, pf

DIEMER, LOUIS (1843-1919)
    Serenade   Heugel   V, fl, pf

DIEPENBROCK, ALPHONS (1862-1921)
    Come Raggio di Sol   Donemus   S, bn, cl, fl, hn,
                                           ob

    Wenn ich ihn nur habe (Novalis) "   S, bn, cl, db, fl,
                                           hn, ob d'am

DIJK, JAN VAN (1918-   )
    5 Liederen   Donemus   B, fl, va, vc, 2vn

    Septet   "   S, cl, db, fl, hn,
                                                va, vc, vn

DIMOV, BOJIDAR (1935-   )
    In cantationes II   Modern   S, fl, hp, tpt, va

DINERSTEIN, NORMAN (1937-   )
    Four Settings (Dickinson)   Boosey   S, st qt

DISTLER, HUGO (1908-1942)
    Kleine Sommerkantate   Bärenreiter   SS, st qt

DOHL, FRIEDHELM (1936-   )
    7 Haiku   Gerig   S, fl, pf

DONIZETTI, GAETANO (1797-1848)
    Ah, che il destino   Univ of Iowa,   SAT, pf
                                 1971, Boyd

    Un hiver à Paris   BPL   1-2V, pf
    5 L'addio ("Dunque addio...")   MsBar, pf
    * Nos 1-4 for V, pf

    J'aime trop pour être heureux Rarities, 1981   S, pf, va

    Matinée Musicale   BPL   2-4V, pf
    6 La gelosia   SB, pf
    7 L'addio   SB, pf
    9 La Campana   TTBB, pf
    10 Rataplan   TTBB, pf
    * Nos 1-5, 8 for V, pf

    Nuits d'été à Pausilippe   "   lowVhiV, pf
      (It/Ger)
    7 Il giuramento (Palazzolo)
    8 L'aurora (Tarantini)
    9 L'alito di Bice (F. Puoti)
    10 Amor voce del Cielo
    11 Un guardo ed una voce
       (Palazzolo)
    12 I Bevitori (Tarantini)
    * Nos 1-6 for V, pf

    Soirées d'automne à   "   1-2V, pf
      l'Infrascata
    5 Il fiore   ST, pf
    * Nos 1-4 for V, pf

DOPPELBAUER, JOSEPH FRIEDRICH (1918-   )
    3 Songs   Doblinger   S, fl, pf, va, vc

DORATI, ANTAL (1906-   )
    The Two Inchantments of   Zerboni   Bar, 3fl, hn, hp,
      Li-Tai-Po   2perc

DRESDEN, SEM (1881-1957)
    4 Vocalises   Donemus   Ms, bn, cl, fl,
                                                        perc, pf, va, vn

DRUCKMAN, JACOB (1928-   )
    Animus II   MCA   Ms(S), 2perc, tp

    Dark upon the Harp (Psalms)   Presser   Ms, hn, 2perc,
                                                        2tpt, trbn, tuba

DUPARC, HENRI (1848-1933)
    Benedicat vobis Dominus   Salabert (LC)   STB, org

DUREY, LOUIS (1888-1979)
    Images à Crusoe (Perse)   Chester, 1922   V, cel, cl, fl, st
                                                        qt

DVORAK, ANTONIN (1841-1904)
19a O Sanctissima   Artia   ABar, org

20   Moravské dvojzpevy   AD, vi/3,   ST, pf
   1 Promeny   Bärenreiter,
   2 Rozlouceni   Schott
   3 Chudoba
   4 Vure suhaj, vure

32   Moravské dvojzpevy   AD, vi/3,   SA, pf
   1 A ja ti uplynu   Simrock
   2 Velet, vtacku
   3 Dyby byla kosa nabrosena
   4 V dobrym sme se sesli
   5 Slavikovksy polecko maly
   6 Holub na javore
   7 Voda a plac
   8 Skromna
   9 Prsten
  10 Zelenaj se, zelenaj
  11 Zajata
  12 Neveta
  13 Sipek
  14 Zivot vojensky
   * first 5 pieces orig op. 29

38   Moravské dvojzpevy   AD, vi/3,   SA, pf
   1 Moznost   Bärenreiter,
   2 Jablko   Schauer
   3 Venecek
   4 Hore

Ruské pisne (Czech/Rus)	AD, vii	2V, pf
1 Povylétla holubice pode strani		
2 Cim jsem ja te rozhnevala		
3 Mlada, pekna krasavice		
4 Cozpak, muj holoubku		
5 Zkvétal, zkvétal v maj i kvet		
6 Jako mhou se tmi		
7 Ach, vy ricky sumivé		
8 Mladice ty krasna		
9 Po matusc, mosné Volze		
10 Na policku briza tam stala		
11 Vyjdu ja si podle ricky		
12 Na tom nasem namesti		
13 Ja si zasil bez orani		
14 Y, ty lucni kacko mala		
15 V poli zraji visne		
16 Oj, Krace Lauran cerny		
Na tei nasej strese lastovecka	AD, vi	SA, pf

EBEN, PETR (1929–)

Pisne Nejtajnejsi (Czech/Ger)	Panton	A, va, opt pf
Sestero Piesni Milostnych (Czech/Ger/Eng/Fr/It)	Supraphon	medV, hp(pf)
Tri tiché pisne (Czech/Ger)	Czech	S, fl, pf

EDWARDS, GEORGE (1943–)

3 Hopkins Songs	ACA	SS, 2pf
Veined Variety (Hopkins)	Mobart, 1978	S, cl/bcl, fl/pic, vc, vn
Wild Air (Hopkins)	ACA, 1975	A, 4rec

EGK, WERNER (1901–1983)

La Tentation de St Antoine (after 18th c verse)	Schott	A, st qt

EINEM, GOTTFRIED VON (1918–)

Geistliche Sonate	Boosey	S, org, tpt

EL-DABH, HALIM (1921–)

Tahmeela (Eng)	Peters	S, bn, cl, fl, hn, ob, vn
1 Benighted is the Night		
2 Oh! Vista		
3 Pale in the Shadow		

EMMANUEL, MAURICE (1862-1938)
        In Memoriam (Vallery-Radot)   Durand   hiV, pf, vc, vn

        Trois Odelettes Anacréontiques   "   V, fl, pf

ERDMANN, DIETRICH (1917-   )
        Gesänge des Abschieds (Jiménez) Breitkopf   hiV, fl, pf

ERLEBACH, PHILIPP HEINRICH (1657-1714)
        Heute Ist der Siegestag   Hänssler   hiV, bc, 2rec

        Ich kasse Gott in allem Walten   "   hiV, bc, 2rec

        Ihr Gedanken (Ger/Eng)   Bote   S(T), kbd, 2vn

ERLICH, ABEL
        The Writing of Hezekiah   Isr Mus Inst   S, bn, ob, vn

ESTEVE, PIERRE (1720-1779)
        Fortunita, fortunita   UME   ST, pf

FALLA, MANUEL DE (1876-1946)
        Psyché (Jean-Aubry)   Chester   S, fl, hp, va, vn

        Soneto A Cordoba   "   hiV, hp(pf)
          (L. de Gongora) (Sp/Eng)

FARKAS, FERENC (1905-   )
        Tibicinium (A. Keleti)   Boosey   V, fl
          (Hung/Ger)

FAURE, GABRIEL (1845-1924)
  10   1 Puisqu'ici-bas (Hugo)   Hamelle   SS, pf
        2 Tarantelle (Monnier)   "

  43   Nocturne   Salabert, 1886   S, fl, pf

  54   Ecce fidelis servus   Hamelle (HL)   STB, db, org

  65   1 Ave Verum   EC Schirmer, 1954 SA, org

  72   Pleurs d'or (Samain)   Hamelle   AB, pf

  93   Ave Maria   Heugel (NYPL)   SS, harm, vc, vn

FELDMAN, MORTON (1926-   )
        For Franz Kline   Peters, 1962   S, chim/pf, hn, vc,
                                                   vn

Intervals	Peters, 1961	Bbar, perc, trbn, vc, vib
Journey to the End of Night (Céline)	Peters, 1963	S, bcl, bn, cl, fl
The O'Hara Songs (F. O'Hara)	Peters, 1962	Bbar, chim, pf, va, vc, vn
Rabbi Akiba	Peters, 1963	S, db, eng hn, fl, hn, perc, pf/cel, tuba, tpt, trbn
Four Songs to e.e. cummings	Peters, 1951	S, pf, vc
Vertical Thoughts III	Peters, 1963	S, db, fl, hn, 2 perc, pf/cel, tuba, tpt, trbn, vc, vn
Vertical Thoughts V	"	S, cel, perc, tuba, vn

FELLEGARA, VITTORIA (1927-   )

Epitaphe * 7'30"	Zerboni	SS, fl, perc, pf/cel, timp, vib

FERRARI, GIORGIO (1925-   )

Ai Fratelli Cervi	Sonzogno	Ms(Bar), cl, fl, hp, hn, ob, perc, tpt, trbn, va, vc, vn

FERRITTO, JOHN (1937-   )

9 Oggi	ACA	S, cl, pf

FERRO, STEFANO

Suite Agreste (It/Ger)	Ricordi	fV, cl, eng hn, fl, hp, va

FINE, VIVIAN (1913-   )

The Confession (Racine)	Catamount, 1972	S, fl, pf, va, vc, vn
The Great Wall of China (Kafka) * 4'	Presser	medV(hiV)spkr, fl, pf, vc
A Guide to the Life Expectancy of a Rose (S.R. Tilley)	ACA, Catamount	ST, cl, fl, hp(pf), vc, vn
4 Songs	Presser	medV, st qt
Teisho	Catamount, 1976	8V, st qt

FINKBEINER, REINHOLD (1929-   )
     Epiphanie   Breitkopf-W   SABar, org, 3perc

FLANAGAN, WILLIAM (1923-1969)
     Goodbye My Fancy (Whitman)   Southern Peer,   S, fl, gtr(pf)
                                      1964

     The Lady of Tearful Regret   ACA   colSBar, cl, fl,
       (Albee)   pf, st qt

     The Weeping Pleiades (Hausman)   Southern Peer   Bar, cl, fl, pf,
     * 5'   vc, vn

FLEGIER, ANGE (1846-1927)
     Le Rendez-Vous   Enoch   MsBar, pf

FLOTHIUS, MARIUS (1914-   )
34   Love and Strife (Raine)   Donemus   A, fl, ob, va, vc

49   Negro Lament (L. Hughes)   "   A, [arec(asax)
                                     (ob)(va)](pf)

60   Odysseus und Nausikad (Homer)   "   SATBar, spkr, hp

FOOTE, ARTHUR (1853-1937)
     Come, live with Me   NEC   SA, pf

     Love is a bubble   "   S(T), pf, vn

     Sing, maiden, sing   "   SB, pf

     A Song from the Persian   "   SA, pf

     The sun is low   "   S(T), pf, vn

     The Voice of Spring   "   SA, pf

FORTNER, WOLFGANG (1907-   )
     Mitte des Lebens (Hölderlin)   B Schott   S, bcl, fl, hn, hp,
                                     vn

FOSS, LUKAS (1922-   )
     3 Airs for Frank O'Hara's   Salabert   S(Ct), va(vc), hpd,
       Angel   pf

     Time Cycle   C Fischer   S, cl, perc,
     * 4'   pf/cel, vc

FOSTER, STEPHEN (1826-1864)
     America's Bicentennial Songs   G Schirmer, 1975,   1-4V, pf(gtr)
                                     ed Gregg Smith

     Ellen Bayne   TB, pf(gtr)

Little Mac, little Mac		SATB, pf
Some folks		SATB, pf(gtr)
Somebody's coming to see me tonight		SATB, pf
The voices that are gone		SATB, pf
We are coming, Father Abraam		SATB, pf
The White House Chair		SATB
Willie has gone to the war		SATB, pf
Household Songs	DaCapo, 1973	1-4V, pf
Come where my love lies dreaming		SATB
Gentle Lena Clare		SATB, pf
Happy Hours at home		SATB, pf
Mr. and Mrs. Brown		MsBar, pf
Wilt thou be gone, love?		ST, pf
Minstrel-show Songs	DaCapo, 1980	1-4V, pf
Angelina Baker		SATB, pf
Dolly Day		SATB, pf
Farewell my Lilly dear		TB, pf
Gwine to run all night!		SATB, pf
Jenny June		SATB, pf
Melinda May		SATB, pf
My brodder Gum		SATB, pf
My old Kentucky Home		SATB, pf
Nelly Bly		SA, pf
Nelly was a lady		SATB, pf
Oh! Lemuel		SATB, pf
Oh! Susanna		SATB, pf
Old Black Joe		SAB, pf
A soldier in the colored brigade		SATB, pf

FRANCK, CESAR (1822-1890)

89	Six Duos	Enoch	SA, pf

1 L'ange gardien
2 Aus petits enfants (A. Daudet)
3 La Vierge à la crèche (Daudet)
4 Les danses de Lormont (Desbordes-Valmore)
5 Soleil G. Ropartz)
6 La Chanson du Vannier (A. Theuriet

FROIDEBISE, PIERRE (1914-1962)

Amercoeur; petite cantate sur les noms de rues de la ville Liège (Seaux)	CeBeDeM	S, bn, cl, fl, hn, ob/eng hn, pf

FROMM, HERBERT (1905-   )

Chamber Cantata (J. Halevi)	Transcon, 1966	SATB, bn, cl, fl, hn, ob, pf, va, vn
Yemenite Cycle	Israeli	medV, fl, hp, perc

FURSTENAU, ANTON BERNHARD (1792–1852)
117   Souvenir de Maxen   Bote   S, fl, pf

139   An die erste Lerche   Breitkopf   S, fl, pf

141   Liebesruf   Fürstner   S, fl, pf

           L'Amant, Romance   "   S, fl, pf

FUSSAN, WERNER (1912–   )
           Die chinesische Flöte   Breitkopf-W   S, fl, st qt
           (Li-Tai-Pe)

FUSSL, KARL HEINZ (1924–   )
           Miorita   Universal   T(S), cl/bcl,
                                                          fl/afl, pf/cel, vc,
                                                          vn/va

GALVAN, VENTURA (fl. 1762–73)
           Los Vagamundos y ciegos finidos UME   SST, pf

GARCIA, MANUEL (1775–1832)
           El Majo y la Maja   "   2V, pf

GAUBERT, PHILIPPE (1879–1941)
           Soir paien   Enoch   V, fl,pf

GERHARD, ROBERTO (1896–1970)
           The Akond of Swat (Lear)   Oxford   S, perc

           5 Songs   Prowse   S, fl, pf

GERSTBERGER, KARL THEODOR (1892–1955)
   12   Kammerkantate (Wunderhorn)   Breitkopf, 1928   SS, cl, 2fl

GIDEON, MIRIAM (1906–   )
           The Adorable Mouse   G Schirmer   V, bn, cl, fl, hpd,
           (La Fontaine)   timp

           The Condemned Playground   Bomart   ST, bn, fl, st qt
           (Horace, Milton, Baudelaire)

           The Hound of Heaven   Galaxy   V, ob, st tr
           (F. Thompson)

           Nocturnes (Shelley,   Bomart   S, fl, ob, vc, vib,
           Untermeyer, F. Sherman)   vn

           Questions on Nature (Adelard   "   V, glk, ob, pf, tam
           of Bath)

Rhymes from the Hill (Morgenstern)	Bomart	V, cl, mar, vc
The Seasons of Time (ancient Jap Tanka poetry)	General	V, fl, pf/cel, vc
3 Sonnets from "Fatal Interview" (Millay)	ACA	V, va, vc(pf), vn
5 Sonnets from Shakespeare	"	lowV(hiV), tpt, st qt
Spiritual Madrigals (Rilke, Heine, von Trimperg)	"	2 or 3maleV, bn, vc, vn

GINASTERA, ALBERTO (1916–   )

Cantata para America Magica (de Toro) (Sp/Eng)	Barry	DramS, 11perc
Cantos del Tucaman (R.J. Sanchez)	Ricordi	S, fl, hp, 2perc, vn

GLANVILLE-HICKS, PEGGY (1912–   )

Letters from Morocco (Paul Bowles)	Peters	T, bn, fl, hp

GLETLE, JOHANN MELCHIOR (1626–1683)

Geistliche Gesänge I	Bärenreiter	ATB, bc
Geistliche Gesänge II	"	S(T), bc, 2vn

GLINKA, MIKHAIL (1804–1857)

Bozhe sil vo dni smyateniya	G, ix	ATB, pf
Come di gloria al nome	"	SATB, st qnt
Kolîbel'naya pesnya	"	A, st qnt
Mio ben ricordati	"	AT, pf
Molitva	"	SATB, pf
Ne iskushay menya bez nuzhdî (E. Baratinsky)	"	ST, pf
La notte omai s'appressa	G, xvii	SATB, st qt
Proshchal'naya pesnya	G, x	TTB, pf
Sogna chi crede d'esser felice	G, ix	ATTB, st qnt
Somneniye (Kukolnik)	"	A, hp, vn
Vî ne pridyote vnov (comp)	"	SS, pf

GOEHR, ALEXANDER (1932-   )
    The Deluge (after da Vinci)   Schott   SA, db, fl, hn, hp,
                                                           tpt, va, vc, vn

GOLDMAN, RICHARD FRANKO (1910-   )
    My Kingdom   Mercury   medV, pf, st tr

GOUNOD, CHARLES (1818-1893)
    Ave Maria   Doblinger, Schott   V, org, vn

    15 Duos   Choudens   ST, pf

GRAENER, PAUL (1872-1944)
113   3 Gedichte   Bote   medV, vc

GRAINGER, PERCY (1882-1961)
    Bold William Taylor   BFMS   V, 1(2)cl, harm,
                                                           6st

    Colonial Song   S   ST, pf tr(pf)

    Died for Love   BFMF   S(A),[bn, cl, fl]
                                                           [va, vc, vn(fl)]
                                                           [pf]

    Early One Morning   "   S, bn, fl, hn,
                                                           st(pf)

    Husband and Wife   DFMS   2V, 2gtr, timp,
                                                           vc(db)

    The Lonely Desert-man Sees the   RMTB   STB, [cl, cl(bn)]
        Tents of the Happy Tribes   (pf)

    Lord Maxwell's Goodnight   BFMS   T, 4st

    The Old Woman at the   DFMS   V, harm, pf
        Christening

    The Power of Love   "   S, var comb inst

    Random Round   RMTB   SAT, gtr, mar, uk,
                                                           va, xyl

    Under a Bridge   DFMS   SB, fl, pf 4hnds,
    * tuneful perc means glk,   tpt, tuneful perc
      hnd bells, tub bells, metal
      and wooden mar, and xyl

    Willow, willow   OEPM   V, (gtr, st qt)(pf)

GRANADOS, ENRIQUE (1867-1916)
    Las Curratacus Modestas   UME   SA, gtr

GREBER, JAKOB (d. 1731)
        Cantata da camera   Kistner   B, bc, fl

GRECHANINOV, ALEXANDER (1864-1956)
  52   3 Mertvîye list'ya   Zimmermann   V, st qt

  62   Zwei Duette (Ger/Russ)   Zimmermann, 1913 SA, pf
        1 Bei Sonnen
        2 Mittagsschwule
        3 Untergang

 131   Deux Mélodies (Tuttchev) B Schott, 1934   S, hp, vc
        1 Un jour d'été
        2 Dernier amour

GRETRY, ANDRE-ERNEST (1741-1813)
        Céphale et Proxis   Zimmermann   S, fl, pf
        * recit and aria

GRIESBACH, KARL-RUDI (1916)
        Nacht der Farben   Breitkopf   S, hp, 5st

GRIMM, HEINRICH (1593-1637)
        2 Kleine geistliche Konzerte Bärenreiter   MsMs(BarBar), bc

        2 Kleine Osterkonzerte   "   MsMs(BarBar), bc

        2 Kleine Weihnachtskonzerte   "   SS, bc

GRUENBERG, LOUIS (1884-1964)
  21   The Daniel Jazz (Lindsay) Universal   medV, cl, perc, pf,
                                                 tpt, va, vc, 2vn

  23   The creation (after Negro   "   V, bn(vc), cl, fl,
          spiritual)   hn, perc, pf, timp,
                                               va

GUACCERO, DOMENICO (1927-   )
        Studio per un quartetto   Bruzzichelli   ST, cl, tsax

GUEZEC, JEAN PIERRE (1934-1971)
        Couleurs Juxtaposées II   Salabert, 1971   ST
        * 6'

GUGLIELMI, PIETRO ALESSANDRO (1728-1804)
        Terzetto Adalinda   Carisch   hiVmedV, 2cl

GURSCHING, ALBRECHT (1934-   )
        Anakreontika   Modern   Bar, bn, fl, 2perc

HALFFTER, CRISTOBAL (1930–   )
    4 Brecht Lieder   Universal   medV, 2pf

    Noch'e passiva del sentido   "   S, 2perc

HAMBRAEUS, BENGT (1928–   )
    Gacelas y casidas (Lorca)   Nordiska   T, bcl, cel, eng
                                                                   hn, fl, perc, vib

34   Spectogram   "   S, fl, 4gongs, vib

HAMERIK, ASGER (1843–1923)
    Nocturne   Breitkopf, 1897   Ms, db, fl, st qt

HAMILTON, IAIN (1922–   )
    Nocturnal (Donne)   Schott   SSSSAATTBBB

    Songs of Summer   "   hiV, (cl, pf, vc)
                                                                   (pf)

HAMMERSCHMIDT, ANDREAS (1611–1675)
    Ander Theil Weltlicher Oden   EDM, 1962   1–3V, vn, gam
      oder Liebesgesange

    Dritter Theil geist–und   "   1–5V, bc
      weltlicher Oden und
      Madrigalen

    Erster Theil Weltlicher Oden   "   1–2V, gam, vn
      oder Liebesgesang

    Es danken dir Gott die Völker   Bärenreiter   T, bc, 2vn

    Zwei Geistliche Konzerts   Hänssler   SS(TT), bc

HANDEL, GEORGE FRIDERIC (1685–1759)
    A miravi io son intento   HG, xxxii   SA, bc

    Ahi, nelle sorte umane   "   SS, bc

    Amor gioje mi porge   "   SS, bc

    Beato in ver che puo (after   "   SA, bc
      Horace)

    Caro autor di mia doglia   "   ST(SS)(AA), bc

    Che vai pensando   "   SB, bc

    Conservate, raddoppiate   Gerig   SA, bc

    Fronda leggiera e mobile   HG, xxxii   SA, bc

    Giu nei tartarei regni   "   SB, bc

Langue, geme e sospira	HG, xxxii	SA, bc
Nell Dolce dell'Oblio	B Schott	S, bc, fl
No, di voi non vuo fidarmi	HG, xxxii	SS(SA), bc
Quando in calma ride il mare	"	SB, bc
Quel fior ch'all'alba nasce	"	SSB, bc
Quel fior ch'all'alba ride	"	SSB, bc
Quel fior ch'all'alba ride	"	SS, bc
Salve Regina	G Schirmer	S, org, vc, 2vn
Se tu non lasci amore	HG, xxxii	SSB, bc
Se tu non lasci amore	"	SA, bc
Sono liete, fortunate	"	SA, bc
Tacete, ohime tacete	"	SB, bc
Tanti strali al Sen	"	SA, bc
Troppo cruda	"	SA, bc
Va, speme infida	"	SS, bc

HARRIS, ROGER (1940-   )

Caliban in Apartment 112	Seesaw	T, perc, pf, sax, vib

HARRIS, ROY (1898-1979)

Abraham Lincoln Walks at Midnight (Lindsay)	AMP	Ms, pf tr
Lamentation	Belwin, 1981	S, pf, va

HARRISON, LOU (1917-   )

Alma Redemptoris Mater	Southern Peer	Bar, pf, trbn, vn

HART, PHILIP (1703-1749)

Proceed, sweet charmer of the ear	Schott	SS, bc, 2rec

HARTIG, HEINZ (1907-1969)

16 Der Trinker und der Spiegel (Mehring)	Bote	Bar, cl, db, fl, perc, pf, pic, tpt, va

HARTLEY, WALTER (1927-   )
    A Psalm Cycle   Tri-ten   med-hiV, fl, pf

HARVEY, JONATHAN (1939-   )
    Angel/Eros (comp)   Novello   hiV, st qt

    Black Sonnet (Hopkins, comp)   "   SMsBarB, bn, cl,
                                                                    fl, hn, ob

HASSE, JOHANN FRIEDRICH (1902-   )
    Das Gesprach mit Nikodemus   Sirius   Bar, cl, fl, st qt

    Pallido il Sole   Broekmans   A, pf, vc, vn

HAUDEBERT, LUCIEN (1877-1963)
    3 Evocations   Eschig, 1926   V,[fl(pf)][fl, st
                                                                    qt]

HAUFRECHT, HERBERT (1909-   )
    Let's Play Maccabees   ACA   medV, cl, hp, ob,
                                                                    perc

HAWKINS, JOHN (1944-   )
    3 Cavatinas   Berandol   S, cel, vc, vib, vn

HAYDN, JOSEF (1732-1808)
    Two Italian Duets (Badini)   Doblinger, 1959   ST, pf
      Guarda qui che lo vedrai
      Saper vorrei se m'ami

    Partsongs: Bärenreiter, 1971   3-4voices, pf(bc)
    1 Der Augenblick (Gotz)   SATB, pf
    * 2'45"
    2 Die Harmonie in der Ehe (Gotz)   SATB, pf
    * 2'
    3 Alles hat seine Zeit   SATB, pf
    * 1'30"
    4 Die Beredsamkeit (G.E. Lessing)   SATB, pf
    5 Der Greis (J.W.L. Gleim)   SATB, pf
    * 3'
    6 An den Vetter (Weisse)   STB, pf
    7 Daphens einziger Fehler   TTB, pf
      (Ramler)
    8 Die Warnung   SATB, pf
    9 Betrachtung des Todes   SAT, pf
    10 Wider den ubermut   SATB, pf
    11 An die Frauen (Anacreon)   TTB, pf
    12 Aus dem Danklied zu Gott   SATB, pf
      (Gellert)
    13 Abendlied zu Gott   SATB, pf

    Schotische Lieder   HW, xxxii   V, pf, vn

    350 folksong arr.   HL   1-4V, pf tr

HAYDN, MICHAEL (1737-1806)
    Gott, ich falle dir zur Füssen   Böhm   S, org, vn

HAZZARD, PETER (1949-   )
    Massage   Seesaw   SAB, cl, fl, flug
                                                            hn, 3perc, tsax,
                                                            trbn

HEAD, MICHAEL (1900-1976)
    Bird Song   Boosey   S, fl, pf

    A Piper (O'Sullivan)   Boosey, 1923   hiV, fl, pf

HEIDER, WERNER (1930-   )
    Commission (Pound)   Peters   Bar, 10 inst

    Picasso-Musik (Picasso)   "   Ms, cl, pf, vn

HEINICHEN, JOHANN DAVID (1683-1729)
    Nisi Dominus Aedificaverit   Deutscher   hiV, bc, ob
      Dominum (Psalm 127)

HEISS, HERMANN (1897-1966)
    7 dreistimmige Sentenzen nach Breitkopf   SABar, pf(3st)
      Worten von Günther Michael

    7 Galgenlieder (Morgenstern)   Müller, 1955   S, fl

    Zum neuen Jahr. 7 Erich   Breitkopf   S, cl, pf
      Kastner aphorisms

HEISS, JOHN (1938-   )
    Songs of Nature   Boosey, 1978   Ms, cl, fl, pf, vc,
                                                            vn

HELDER, BARTHOLOMAEUS (1585-1625)
    Dich bitt ich, trautes Jesulein Hänssler   hiV, bc, 2rec

HENSCHEL, SIR GEORGE (1850-1934)
  4   Drei Duette   Schlesinger   SS(TT), pf
    1 Kein Feuer, keine Kohle
    2 Es Weiss und Rath es doch
      keiner (Eichendorff)
    3 Gute Lehre

 33   1 Sehr langsam   Bote   SA(TB), pf
    2 Langsam und traumerlich
    3 Sehr lebhaft

 60   Drei Lieder für zwei   Simrock, 1903   MsT, pf
      Singstimmen

    1 Sommer-Abend (Schantz)
    2 Herbstgefuhl (Gerock)
    3 Erster-Schnee (Keller)

HENSEL, WALTER (1887-1956)
    Mondlieder   Bärenreiter   V, fl, lute

HENZE, HANS WERNER (1926-   )
    Apollo et Hyazinthus (Trakl)   Schott, 1957   A, bn, cl, fl, hn,
                                                              hpd, st qt

    Ariosi (Tasso)   Schott   S, pf 4hnds, vn

    Being Beauteous (Rimbaud) (Fr)   "   S, hp, 4vc

    El Cimarron (Barnet-   Schott, 1972   B, spkr, fl, gtr,
      Enzensberger)   perc
    * 1 hr 16'

    Kammermusik (Hölderlin)   Schott   T, bn, cl, hn,
                                                              gtr(hp), st qnt

    Wiegenlied der Mutter Gottes   "   S, cl, db, fl, hn,
                                                              hp, tpt, trbn, va,
                                                              vc

HERMAN, FRIEDRICH
  38   Chinese Suite (after Bethge's   Breitkopf   S, vc
      Chinesische Flöte)

HESSENBERG, KURT (1908)
  64   7 Leben möcht ich haben   Bärenreiter   A, arec, fl, va,
                                                              vc, vn

    Elizabeth   Peters   Ms, pf, vn

    10 Lieder   Schott   Ms(Bar), pf, va, vn

HINDEMITH, PAUL (1895-1963)
  23   Die Junge Magd (Trakl)   B Schott, 1949   A, cl, fl, st qt
    1 Oft am Brunnen
    2 Stille schafft sie in der
      Kammer
    3 Nächtens Übern kahlen Anger
    4 In der Schmiede dröhnt der
      Hammer
    5 Schmächtig hingestreckt im
      Bette
    6 Abends schweben blutige Linnen
    * 6'

  23a   Des Todes Tod (Reinacher)   B Schott   Ms, 2va, 2vc
    1 Gesicht von Tod und Elend
    2 Gottes Tod

```
            3 Des Todes Tod
              * 3'

   35        Die Serenaden              B Schott          S, ob, va, vc
            1 Barcarole (A. Licht)
            2 An Phyllis (J.W.L. GLeim)
            3 Nur Mut (L. Tieck)
            4 duet                                        vc, va
            5 Der Abend (Eichendorff)
            6 Der Wurm am Meer (J.W. Meinhold)
            7 trio                                        ob, va, vc
            8 Gute Nacht (S. A. Mahlmann)


HODDINOTT, ALUN (1929-    )
   54        Roman Dream (Humphreys)    Oxford            S, cel, hp, perc, pf
              * scena


HOEREE, ARTHUR (1897-    )
    3        Septet                     Eschig, 1932      Ms, fl, pf, st qt


HOLLIGER, HEINZ (1939-    )
             Cantata.  Erde und Himmel  Schott, 1963      T, fl, hp, va, vc,
               (Gwerder)                                  vn

             Glühende Rätsel (N. Sachs) Schott            A, bcl, cimb, fl,
                                                          hp, mar, perc, va


HOLLOWAY, ROBIN (1943-    )
    3        3 Poems (Empson)           Oxford            Ms, cl/bcl, db,
                                                          fl/pic/afl, hpd,
                                                          7perc


HOLST, GUSTAV (1874-1934)
   35        Four songs                 Chester, 1920     V, vn
            1 Jesu sweet, now will I sing
               to Thee
            2 My soul has brought but fire
               and ice
            3 I sing for a maiden that
               matchless is
            4 My leman is so true


HOLST, IMOGEN (1907-    )
             6 Shakespeare Songs        Faber             B, 3rec


HONEGGER, ARTHUR (1892-1955)
             Trois Chansons (Ronsard)   Salabert          V, fl, st qt
               Chanson des Sirènes
               Berceuse de la Sirène
               Chanson de la Poire

             4 Chansons                 Senart, 1924      V, fl, st qt
```

HOPKINS, BILL (1943-   )
          2 Poems (Joyce)   Universal   S, bcl, hp, tpt, va

HORST, ANTON VAN DER (1899-1965)
          3 Oud-Nederlandsche Liederen   Alsbach, 1932   V, fl, org(pf)

HORVATH, JOSEPH MARIA (1931-   )
          Die Blinde (Melodrama after   Peters   A, 2spkr, fl, pf,
            Rilke)   tpt, vc

          Vier Lieder (Hölderlin)   "   S(T), cl, fl, va, vc

HOSSEIN, AMINOULLAH
          Chant de Chamelier   Enoch   V, fl, pf

HOVHANESS, ALAN (1911-   )
  56   4 Hercules   Peters   S, vn
          *5'

 139   O Lady Moon (Lafcadio Hearn)   Marks, New Vistas   hiV, cl, pf
                                         in Song

 169   Live in the Sun   Peters   V, cel
          * 2'

 243   Saturn   "   S, cl, pf
          * 24' 30"

HOVLAND, EGIL (1924-   )
  44   Magnificat   Norsk   A, afl, hp

HUBER, KLAUS (1924-   )
          Auf die ruhige Nacht Zeit   Bärenreiter, 1961   S, fl, va, vc
            (C.R. von Greiffenberg)

          Des Engels Anredung an die   Universal   T, cl, fl, hn, hp
            Seele (J.G. Albini)

HUE, GEORGES-ADOLPHE (1858-1948)
          Chansons lointaines
          4 Soir paien   Salabert   V, fl, pf
          * 2'45"
          * first 3 songs for V, pf

HUFSCHMIDT, WOLFGANG (1934-   )
          Ich steh an deiner Krippen   Bärenreiter   ST, vc, 2vn
            hier
          * Christmas

HUGGLER, JOHN (1928-   )
 20   For Coloratura, Clarinet,   ACA   colS, cl, va, vc
            Viola, Cello

HUGHES, HERBERT (1882-1937)
         Three satirical songs   Enoch   V, bn, cl, fl, vn

HUNFF, JOHANN NICOLAUS (1665-1711)
         Ich will den Herrn loben   Bärenreiter   S, bc, vn

IBERT, JACQUES (1890-1962)
         Aria   Leduc, 1932   Ms, fl, pf
         * vocalise, 4'

         Deux Stèles Orientées   Heugel, 1926   S, fl
            (Segalen)

IPPOLITOV-IVANOV, MICHAEL (1859-1935)
         Chetyre stikhotvoreniia   LC   hiV, fl, pf
            Rubindranata Tagora
            I ruki l'nut k rukam
            Zhelten'kaia ptichka
            Ne ukhodi ne prostivshis'
               so mnoi
            O, moi drug, vot svetok

IRELAND, JOHN (1879-1962)
         At Early Dawn in Summer Woods   Curwen   SA, pf

IVES, CHARLES (1874-1921)
         For you and Me   Schirmer   TTBB, pf

         Sunrise   Peters, 1977   medV, pf, vn
         * 5'30"

IVEY, JEAN EICHELBERGER (1924-   )
         Hera, Hung from the Sky   AMC   Ms, bn, cel, cl,
                                                               fl, hn, ob, perc,
                                                               pf, pic, timp, tpt,
                                                               trbn, tp

         Prospero (Shakespeare)   C Fischer   B, hn, perc, tp
         * 9'

         Solstice   "   S, fl/pic, perc, pf
         * 13'

         3 Songs of Night   "   S, afl, cl, pf,
         * 14'   tp, va, vc

         Songs of Pan   AMC   A, rec(fl), pf

JACOB, GORDON (1895–   )
    Three Songs   Oxford   S, cl
    1 Of all the birds that I do
      know
    2 Flow my tears (Dowland)
    3 Ho, who comes here (Morley)

    Songs of Innocence (Blake)   HMA   S, st tr

JADASSOHN, SALOMON (1831–1902)
72   9 Folk Songs (Ger/Eng)   Breitkopf (NEC)   SA(TB), pf
    1 Wär ich ein Vogelein
    2 Mein Herz thut mir gar zu weh
    3 Frühlingsglaube (Uhland)
    4 Frische Fahrt (Eichendorff)
    5 Treue Liebe (Goethe)
    6 Haidenröslein (Goethe)
    7 Im Volkston (Storm)
    8 Gode Nacht (Storm)
    9 So viel Stern' am Himmel
      stehen (Wunderhorn)
    * Eng trans auth by comp

JANACEK, LEOS (1854–1928)
    Diary of One Who Vanished   Bärenreiter   ST, pf

    Kinderreime (Rikadla)   Universal, 1928   hiV/8V, pf, vn(va)
    (Ger/Eng/Czech)

JEFFREYS, GEORGE (1610–1685)
    Heu, me miseram   Novello   SB, bc
    * Christmas

JELINEK, HANNS (1901–1969)
28   Unterwegs   Modern   S, db, vib
    * cantata

JENSCH, LOTHAR
    Notturno scordato   Breitkopf   V, fl, vc

JEPPESEN, KNUD (1892–1974)
    Domino refugium factum est   Hansen   S, fl, vn
    * cantata

JEZ, JAKOB (1928–   )
    Spomin   G Schirmer   V, glk, pf

JOHNSON, ROBERT SHERLAW (1932–   )
    Green Whispers of Gold   Oxford   S, pf, tp

	The Praises of Heaven and Earth (Psalm cxlviii)	Oxford	S, pf, tp

JOHNSON, TOM (1939-   )
	Trio	AMP	S, vc, vib

JOLAS, BETSY (1926-   )
	Mots * 7'	Heugel	SMsCtB, bn, cl, fl, hp, hpd, 2ob, perc
	Quatuor II * 15'30"	"	S, st tr

JOLIVET, ANDRE (1905-1974)
	Madrigal (M. Jacob) * 12'	Boosey, 1967	SATB, bn(vc), eng hn(vn), fl, pic, va (vn)
	Suite liturgigue	Durand, 1947	T(S), eng hn, hp, ob, vc

JOMMELLI, NICCOLO (1714-1774)
	Miserer a due Canti Soli (It/Ger)	Forni	medV, db, va, 2vn

JOSEPHS, WILFRED (1927-   )
47	Four Japanese Lyrics	Novello	hiV, cl, pf

KADOSA, PAL (1903-   )
30	Volksliederkantate	Boosey	V, cl, vc, vn

KAGEL, MAURICIO (1931-   )
	Abend * 6'	Universal, 1975	SSAATTBB, elec org, pf, 5trbn

KALLIWODA, JOHANN WENZEL (1801-1866)
98	In die Ferne	HMA	hiV, pf, vn
117	Heimathlied	Musica Rara, 1982	S, cl, pf

KAMINSKI, HEINRICH (1886-1946)
	3 Sacred Songs	Universal	V, cl, vn

KARG-ELERT, SIGFRID (1877-1933)
87	3 Symphonic Chorale "Nun ruhen alle Wälder"	Breitkopf	medV, org, vn

KARLINS, M. WILLIAM (1932-   )
    Four Inventions and a Fugue   ACA   A, bn, pf

    Song for Soprano   "   S, fl, vc

    Three Songs   Media   S, fl, pf

    Three Songs on 16th, 17th   ACA   S, fl, vc, vn
       Century Poems

KAUDER, HUGO (1888-1972)
    Ten Poems from James Joyce's   Boosey   SAT, st qt
       Chamber Music

KAY, ULYSSES (1917-   )
    3 Pieces after Blake   C Fischer   Ms, pf, vc, vn

KELEMAN, MILKO (1924-   )
    Epitaph   Peters   Ms, 3 perc, va, vib

    Musik für Heissenbüttel   "   Ms, cl, pf, vc, vn

KELTERBORN, RUDOLF (1931-   )
    Elegie   Modern   Ms, cem, ob, perc,
                                               va

    Kana   Bärenreiter   Bar, org, 2vn

KERR, HARRISON (1897-   )
    Carol   ACA   hiV, 4st

    Notations on a Sensitized Plate New Mus Ed   hiV, cl, pf, st qt

KILLMAYER, WILHELM (1927-   )
    Blasons für Soprano   B Schott   S, cl, pf, vc, vn

    Le Petit Savoyard   Modern   S, cem, db, fl,
                                               4perc, pic, vc, vn

KIM, EARL (1920-   )
    Earthlight (Samuel Beckett)   Mobart, 1978   hiS, lights, pf, vn

KING, HAROLD
    A Dialogue from "A Century of   Donemus   Bar, bn(vc), pf
       Roundels"

    Etre Poète   "   S, cl, fl, pf

KOBLER, ROBERT
    5 Wilhelm Busch Lieder   Breitkopf   S, pf, vn

KOCH, FREDERICK (1924-   )
    Trio of Praise   Seesaw   medV, pf, va

KODALY, ZOLTAN (1882-1967)
    Eight Little Duets (Eng/Hung) Boosey, 1958   ST, pf
    1 Thus starts the Kalevala...
    2 Do not for gold and silver...
    3 From the woods a small bird...
    4 My little daughter...
    5 Maiden beauty
    6 Tulip, tulip fully blown...
    7 Maker of the stars above us...
    8 Counting song

KOERPPEN, ALFRED (1926-   )
    Die Vagantenballade (after F. Breitkopf   B, fl, perc, pf
        Villon)

KOLB, BARBARA (1939-   )
    Chanson bas (Mallarmé)   C Fischer, 1972   S, hp, perc
    * 6'

    Songs before an Adieu   Boosey   S, fl/afl, gtr
    1 The Sentences (Robert Pinsky)
    2 Now I lay (e.e. cummings)
    3 Cantata (Howard Stern)
    4 Gluttonous Smoke (Vasko Popa)
    5 L'Adieu (G. Apollinaire)

KOLINSKI, MIECZYSLAW (1901-   )
    6 French Folksongs   Berandol   S, fl, pf

KOUNADIS, ARGHYRIS (1924-   )
    Drei Nochturnes nach Sappho   Modern   S, cel, fl, va, vc,
                                                         vib, vn

    4 Pezzi (Enzensberger)   Tonger   S, fl, pf, vc

    3 Poems (Cavafy)   "   S, cel, fl, gtr, vc

KRENEK, ERNST (1900-   )
  48a   0 Lacrimosa   Universal, 1927   medV, 2bn, 2cl,
        * 3 songs   2fl, hp

  53a   Vier Gesänge   "   Ms, 3cl, fl, hn, tpt

  67a   Durch die Nacht   Universal, 1931   S, 2cl, 2fl, pf,
                                                         tpt, va, vc, 2vn

  91   La Corona (Donne)   Bärenreiter   MsBar, org, perc

  161   Sestina (Ger text by comp) Bärenreiter, 1958   S, fl, gtr, perc,
                                                         pf, tpt, vn

Quintina (Ger text by comp)   Bärenreiter   S, gtr, perc, tp,
* 9'   va, vib, xyl

KRESKY, JEFFREY (1948-   )
    Cantata II (Shakespeare)   ACA, 1971   STB, cl, hp, va, vc

KRIEGER, JOHANN PHILIPP (1649-1725)
    An den Wassern zu Babel   Bärenreiter   STB, bc, 2vn

    Cantate Domino   Hänssler, 1960   S, bc, 2vn

    Ermuntre Dich   McGinnis, 1961   medV, bc, 2ob(fl,
    * Christmas   rec, vn)

    Heut singt die werte   Hänssler, 1969   SB, bc, tpt, 2vn
        Christenheit
    * Easter

    Wo willst du hin, weil's Abend   Concordia   SS(TT), bc
        ist

KROL, BERNHARD (1920-   )
 30   Horati de vino Carmina   Simrock   S(T), hn, pf

 43   Tagzeiten   Schauer   S, vn

        Maria Klar (sacred)   Bosse   S, db, gtr, perc

KROPFREITER, AUGUSTINUS FRANZ (1936-   )
    In Memoriam (Rilke)   Doblinger   S, fl, va, vc

KUHNAU, JOHANN (1660-1722)
    Ich hebe meine Augen auf   Bieler, 1964   A, bc, 2vn
        (Psalm 121)

LACHENMANN, HELMUT FRIEDRICH (1935-   )
    temA   Breitkopf   V, fl, vc

LACHNER, FRANZ PAUL (1803-1890)
    Frauenliebe und Leben   Musica Rara, 1981   S, hn, pf
        (Chamisso)

LACOME, PAUL (1838-1920)
    Estudiantina   Enoch   SMs(TBar), pf

LADERMAN, EZRA (1924-   )
    From the Psalms   Oxford, 1970   S, (cl, fl, pf, vc,
                                                           vn)(pf)

LADMIRAULT, PAUL (1877-1944)
        Dominical (Elskamp)   Jobert   SATB, pf

LALO, EDOUARD (1823-1892)
31   Chant breton (Delpit)   Hamelle,   V, ob(fl), pf
                                   <u>Mélodies</u> (NYPL)

35   Dansons!   "   SMs, pf

        Au fond des halliers (Theuriet)   "   ST, pf

LANZA, ALCIDES (1929-   )
        3 Songs   Boosey   S, bcl, cl, fl,
        * 6'   perc, trbn, vib

LAPARRA, RAOUL (1876-1943)
        La Chasse au Forêt   Enoch   SA(SB), pf

LASERNA, BLAS DE (1751-1816)
        La Beata   UME   ST, pf

        El Majo y la Italiana Fingida   "   ST, pf

LAWES, HENRY (1596-1662) and WILLIAM (1602-1645)
        Dialogues for two voices and   Penn State, 1964
           continuo
        1 Dialogue between a shepherd   ST, bc
          and a nymph
        2 Dialogue on a kiss   ST, bc
        3 Dialogue between Charon and   TB, bc
          Philomel
        4 Dialogue between Daphne and   SB, bc
          Strephon

LECHNER, KONRAD (1911-   )
        Cantica I   Gerig   Ms, inst

        Cantica II   "   S, fl, perc, treb
                                          inst(cem), vc

        Requiem (Lat)   Peters   A, cem(org), db,
                                          eng hn, 2ob, va, vc

LEDUC, JACQUES (1932-   )
20   Sortilèges Africaines   CeBeDeM   medV, asax, perc, pf

LEES, BENJAMIN (1924-   )
        Medea of Corinth (Jeffers)   Boosey   SMsBarBbar, timp,
        * 28'   ww qnt

LEGLEY, VICTOR (1915–   )
  63   Zeng   CeBeDeM   S, st qt (pf)

LEHMANN, LISA (1862–1918)
        In a Persian Garden   G Schirmer   SATB, pf
          (Fitzgerald, after O Khayyam)
          * 28'

        The Daisy Chain   Boosey, 1900
          1 Foreign children (R.L.   SATB, pf
            Stevenson)
          2 Fairies (Anon.)   A, pf
          3 Keepsake Mill (R.L.   Bar, pf
            Stevenson)
          4 If no one ever marries me   S, pf
            (L.A. Tadema)
          5 Stars (R.L. Stevenson)   T, pf
          6 Seeing the World (Anon.)   SATB, pf
          7 The Ship that sailed into   A, pf
            the Sun (W.B. Rands)
          8 The Swing (R.L. Stevenson)   S, pf
          9 Mustard and Cress (N. Gale)   Bar, pf
         10 The Moon (R.L. Stevenson)   T, pf
         11 Thank you very much indeed   SATB, pf
         12 Blind Man's Buff (Anon.)   SATB, pf
            (N. Gale)

LEIBOWITZ, RENE (1913–1972)
  38   Serenade (Hölderlin, Brentano) Bomart   Bar, cl, fl, hn,
                                                    hp, ob, va, vc, vn

  41   Capriccio   "   hiS, cel, cl, fl,
                                                    hpd, perc, va, vc

  46   3 Poems of Georges Limbour   "   S, cl, fl, pf, st tr
         * 5'

  72   String Quartet no. 7   "   B, st qt
         * 12'

  77   Sonnet (cummings)   "   S, cl, fl, hn, vc,
         * 2'   vn

  92   Three Poems of Pierre Reverdy   Bomart, 1976   SATB, pf
         1 Son de cloche
         2 Air
         3 Soleil

LEICHTLING, ALAN (1947–   )
        Canticle I   Seesaw   S, fl

        Two Proverbs   "   A, 3cl

        Psalm 37   "   A, hp, 4perc, pf,
                                                    va, vc, 2vn

Three Songs (Dickinson)	Seesaw	B, vc
Trial and Death of Socrates	"	B, cl, fl, hp

LEO, LEONARDO (1694-1744)
Salve Regina	Bieler, 1960 (Die Kantate, 4)	S, bc, 2vn

LEONCAVALLO, RUGGERO (1857-1919)
Sérénade Française	Choudens	hiV, pf, vn

LERDAHL, FRED (1943-)
Aftermath * 30'	Bomart	SMsBar, bn, 2cl, 2fl, hp, ob, perc, 4st
Eros * 23'	"	Ms, afl, elec db, elec gtr, elec pf, gtr, hp, 2perc, va
Wake (cummings) * 16'	"	S, hp, perc, st tr

LESLIE, HENRY (1822-1896)
Love Trio	Cramer	SAT, pf
Memory	"	SAT, pf

LESSARD, JOHN (1920-)
5 Poems of John Herrick	ACA	Ms, pf, vn

LEVY, FRANK (1930-)
Specks of Light	Seesaw	S, fl, hn, hp, va, vc, vn

LEWKOVITCH, BERNARD (1927-)
Cantata Sacra (Lat)	Hansen	T, bn, cl, eng hn, fl, trbn, vc
3 Orationes (Lat)	"	T, bn, ob

LIGETI, GYORGY (1923-)
Aventures * 11'	Peters, 1964	colSABar, db, fl, hn, hpd, perc, pf, vc
Nouvelles aventures * 12'30"	Peters, 1966	colSABar, db, fl, hn, hpd, perc, pf, vc

LISZT, FRANZ (1811-1886)
            O Meer im Abendstrahl (Alfred   CW, vii/3   SA, pf(harm)
               Meisner)

LOEFFLER, CHARLES MARTIN (1861-1935)
     5   Quatre poèmes   Schirmer (LC)   Ms, pf, va
            1 La cloche felée (Baudelaire)
            2 "Dansons la gigue!" (Verlaine)
            3 "Le son du cor s'afflige vers
                les bois" (Verlaine)
            4 Sérénade (Verlaine)

            A une femme (Verlaine)   LC   S, pf, vn

LOEWE, CARL (1796-1869)
     88   Gesang der Geister über den   GA, xii   SATB, pf
               Wassern (Goethe)

    104   Drei Duette (Goethe)   "   SS, pf
            1 Die Freude
            2 An Sami
            3 März

            Der Abschied   GA, xvii   SATB, pf

            Liebe rauscht der Silberbach   "   SATB, pf

LOMON, RUTH (1930-   )
            Five Songs after Blake   AMC   lowV, va

            Phase II (Whitman)   "   S, pf, vc

            Songs for a Requiem   "   S, bn, 2cl, fl

LU, YEN (1930-   )
            Concert Piece I   Seesaw   medV, cl, fl, perc,
                                                               vc, vn

LUENING, OTTO (1900-   )
            Hast Never Come to Thee   ACA   S, fl
               (Whitman)
            * 1'

            The Soundless Song   "   S, cl, fl, pf, va,
            * 6'   vc, 2vn

            Suite for Voice and Flute   "   S, fl
            * 8'

            When in the Languor of Evening   "   S, st qt (ww qt), pf
               (Gibbon)

LUTYENS, ELIZABETH (1906-   )
  65   And Suddenly, it's Evening   Schott   T, cel, db, hn, hp,
            (Quasimodo)   perc, 2 tpt, 2 trbn,
                                                            vc, vn

LYBBERT, DONALD (1923-   )
          Lines for the Fallen (Blake)   Peters   S, 2 prep pf
          * 2 pf at quarter-tone

MALIPIERO, GIAN FRANCESCO (1882-1973)
          Dialogho #3 con Jacopone   Ricordi   hiV, 2pf
            da Todi

          4 Vecchie Canzoni   Zerboni   Bar, bn, cl, db,
                                                            fl, hn, ob, va

MALIPIERO, RICCARDO (1914-   )
          In the Time of Daffodils   "   SBar, bcl, db, eng
            (cummings)   hn, fl, gtr, perc,
                                                            va

          6 Poesie di Dylan Thomas   "   S, bcl, fl, hp, ob,
          * 11'   perc, va, vc, 2vn

MAMLOCK, URSULA (1928-   )
          Haiku Settings   ACA, 1967   S, fl

          Five Songs from "Stray Birds"   ACA, 1963   S, fl/afl/pic, vc
            (Tagore)

MARGOLA, FRANCO (1908-   )
          3 Epigrammi Greci   Bongiovanni   hiV, hn, pf

MAROS, RUDOLPH (1917-   )
          Sirato   Southern Peer   medV, 10 inst
          * dif

MARSHALL, PAMELA (1954-   )
          Watchman for the Morning   Seesaw   V, hn, pf

MARTIN, FRANK (1890-1974)
          Trois Chants de Noël (Rudhardt) Universal, 1962   hiV, fl, pf
          1 Les Cadeaux
          2 Image de Noël
          3 Les Bergers

          Quatre Sonnets à Cassandre   Hug, 1939   Ms, fl, va, vc

MARTINU, BOHUSLAV (1890-1959)
      The Primrose   Panton, 1960   SA, pf, vn
      1 A new bonnet
      2 'Bove the farmhouse
      3 Plaint
      4 Good timber
      5 Noonday

MARX, JOSEPH (1882-1964)
      Du bist der Garten   Universal (LC)   medV, pf, vn

      Pan trauert um Syrinx   Universal, 1917   hiV, fl, pf
        (Wildgans)   (LC)

MARX, KARL (1897-   )
23   Reifende Frucht (E. Krauss)   Bärenreiter   SA, pf

38   Frühlingstau in deinen Augen   "   A, pf, rec(fl, vn)

42a   3 Liebeslieder   "   S, st qt

      Da Christus geboren war   "   A, cem, fl, vc, vn

      Vier Lieder (R. Habetin)   "   S, fl, pf

MASSENET, JULES (1842-1912)
      Chansons des Bois d'Amaranthe Heugel   SATB, pf
        (Legrand)
      * 1 duet, 2 trios, 2 qts

      Dialogue Nocturne (Silvestre)   "   ST, pf

      Matinée d'été (C. Distel)   Durand, 1906 (BPL) SSS, pf

      Poème d'amour (Robiquet)   Recital Pub, 1979 ST, pf

      Le Temps et l'Amour (Ludana)   Heugel   TBar, pf

MATHIAS, WILLIAM (1934-   )
63   Ceremony after a Fire Raid Oxford, 1975   SATBarB, perc, pf
        (Dylan Thomas)
      * 20'

MAYER, WILLIAM (1925-   )
      Kartoum   Presser   S, fl, pf, vc, vn

      Miniatures (Dorothy Parker)   "   S, fl, perc, pf,
                                           tpt, vc, vn

McBRIDE, ROBERT (1911-   )
      Commentary   ACA   T, db, drum, pf,
                                         syn, 2tpt, 2trbn

	Nonsense Syllables (Vocalise #3)	ACA	S, fl
	Vocalise	"	S, fl

McNEIL, JAN PFISCHNER (1945-   )

	Aureate Earth	ASUC, 1974	T, perc, pf, prep pf

MELLERS, WILFRED H. (1914-   )

	Ship of Death (Lawrence)	Novello	ST, bcl, cl, st qt

MENDELSSOHN, FANNY (1805-1847)

8	Zuleika und Hatem	Peters, in Felix Mendelssohn, Duette	ST, pf

MENDELSSOHN, FELIX (1809-1847)

63	Sechs Lieder	Peters	SS, pf
	1 Ich wollt' meine Lieb' ergösse sich (Heine)		
	2 Abschiedslied der Zugvögel (Hoffmann von Fallersleben)		
	3 Gruss (Eichendorff)		
	4 Herbstlied (Klingemann)		
	5 Volkslied (R. Burns)		
	6 Maiglöckchen und die Blümelein (Hoffmann von Fallersleben)		

77	Drei Lieder	"	SS, pf
	1 Sonntagsmorgen (Uhland)		
	2 Das Achrenfeld (Hoffmann von Fallersleben)		
	3 Lied aus Ruy Blas (Hugo)		
	Drei Volkslieder	"	hiVlowV, pf
	1 Wie kann ich froh und lustig sein? (P. Kaufmann)		
	2 Abendlied (Heine)		
	3 Wasserfahrt (Heine)		

MERRYMAN, MARJORIE (1951-   )

	Ariel (Shakespeare)	APNM	S, cl, perc, vc
	Laments for Hektor	"	hiSSA, cl, fl, hn, perc, pf, vc, vn

MESSIAEN, OLIVIER (1908-   )

	La mort du nombre	Durand, 1931	ST, pf, vn
	O sacrum convivium	Durand, 1937	SATB, org
	Cinq rechants	Rouart, 1949	SSSAAATTTBBB

MEYERBEER, GIACOMO (1791-1864)
        Hirtenlied (Rellstab)   International,   T(S), cl, pf
                                             1954

MIGOT, GEORGES (1891-1976)
        2 Stèles (Segalen)   Leduc   medV, cel, db, hp,
                                                                perc

MIHALOVICI, MARCEL (1898-   )
        Cantilène   Bieler   Ms, cel, 3cl, fl,
                                                                hps, perc, st

MILHAUD, DARIUS (1892-1974)
   56   Machines Agricoles   Universal, 1954   medV, bn, cl, db,
        * 12'   fl, va, vc, vn

   80   Poèmes de Catulle   Heugel   hiV, vn

   410 Adieu (Rimbaud)   Elkan Vogel, 1965 V, fl, hp, va
        * 9'

        Deux poèmes de Louise de   Heugel, 1956   SATB
          Vilmorin
        1 Fado
        2 L'alphabet des Abeux

        Deux poèmes pour quatuor vocal   Durand, 1923 (BPL) SATB

        Six Sonnets composés au secret   Heugel, 1946   SATB
          par Jean Cassou

        6 Symphonie   Universal, 1956   SATB, ob, vc

MILLER, EDWARD J. (1930-   )
        Mists and Waters   ACA   S, cl, perc, pf, vn

MIROGLIO, FRANCIS (1924-   )
        Magies   Zerboni   S, db, fl, hn, ob,
        * 14'   perc, sax, trbn,
                                                                va, vc, vn

MOLLICONE, HENRY (1946-   )
        2 Love Songs   ACA   T, vn

MONOD, JACQUES-LOUIS (1927-   )
        Chamber Aria (Paul Eluard)   Boelke-Bomart,   S, bn, cl, fl, hn,
                                             1973   ob, pf, tpt

MONTEVERDI, CLAUDIO (1567-1643)
        Madrigali Libro 7   M, vii
          Non è di gentil core   SS, bc

A quest'olmo		SSAATB, bc, 2fl, 2vn
O come sei gentile		SS, bc
Io son pur vezzosetta		SS, bc
O viva fiamma		SS, bc
Vorrei baciarti		AA, bc
Dice la mia bellissima Licori		TT, bc
Ah, che non si conviene		TT, bc
Non vedro mai le stelle		TT, bc
Ecco vicine o bella Tigre		TT, bc
Perchè fuggi		TT, bc
Tornate		TT, bc
Soave libertate		TT, bc
S'el vostro cor Madonna		TB, bc
Interrotte speranze		TTB, bc
Augellin		TTB, bc
Vaga su Spina ascosa		TTB, bc
Eccomi pronta ai baci		SSB, bc
Parlo miser o taccio		SSB, bc
Tu dormi		SATB, bc
Al lume delle stelle		SSTB, bc
Ohimè dov'è il mio ben		2V, bc
Chiome d'oro		2V, bc, 2vn
Con che soavita		V, hpds, lutes, org, st
Amor che deggio far		SSTB, bc, 2vn
Madrigali Libro 8	M, viii	
Altri canti d'Amor		SSATTB, bc, db, gam, 2va, 2vn
Hor ch'el Ciel e la Terra		SSATTB, bc, 2vn
Gira il nemico insidioso		ATB, bc
Ogni amante è guerrier		TT, bc
Riedi		TTB, bc
Ardo avvampo		SSAATTBB, bc, 2vn
Altri canti di Marte		SSATTB, bc, 2vn
Due belli occhi		SSATTTB, bc, 2vn
Vago augeletto		SSATTTB, bc, db, 2vn
Mentre vaga Angioletta		TT, bc
Dell'usate mie corde		TTB, bc
Dolcissimo uscignolo		SSATB, bc
Chi vol haver felice		SSATB, bc
Lamento della Ninfa: Non havea Febo ancora		STTB, bc
Perche t'en fuggi o Fillide		ATB, bc
Non partir ritrosetta		AAB, bc
Su su Pastorelli vezzosi		SSA, bc
Madrigali Libro 9	M, ix	
Bel Pastor		TT, bc
Zefiro torna		TT, bc
Se vittorie si belle		TT, bc
Ardo		TT, bc
O sia tranquillo il mare		ATB, bc
Alcun non mi consigli		ATB, bc
Di far sempre gioire		ATB, bc
Quando dentro al tuo seno		TTB, bc
Non voglio amare		TTB, bc

Come dolce hoggi l'auretta		SSS, bc
Alle danze alle danze		TTB, bc
Perchè se m'odiavi		TTB, bc
Si si ch'io v'amo		TTT, bc
Su su su Pastorelli vezzosi		TTB, bc
O mio bene		TTB, bc
O come vaghi		TTB, bc
Taci Armelin		ATB, bc

Scherzi Musicali a tre voci	M, x	
18 canzonettas:		SS(AT)B, 2vn, vc,
I bei legami		unless otherwise
Amarilli onde m'assale		indicated
Fugge il verno dei dolori		
Quando l'Alba in Oriente		
Non cosi		
Damigella tutta bella		
La Pastorella mia spietata		
O rosetta che rosetta		
Amorosa pupilletta		
Vaghi rai di cigli ardenti		S(SAT)B, vc, 2vn
La violetta		
Giovinetta ritrosetta		
Dolci miei sospiri		
Clori amorosa		
Lidia spina del mio core		
Deh chi tace il bel pensero		
Dispiegate guance amate		
De la Bellezza le dovute lodi		

22 canzonettas	"	3V

MOORE, DOUGLAS (1893-1969)

Ballad of William Sycamore	Galaxy	B, fl, pf, trbn

MORAL, PABLO DEL (fl. 1765-1805)

La Opera Casera	UME	STB, pf
* tornadilla		

MOURET, JEAN-JOSEPH (1682-1738)

Andromède et Persée	Ed Fr Mus, 1973	hiV, bc, vn

MOZART, WOLFGANG AMADEUS (1756-1791)

K A24a	Ach, was mussen wir erfahren	NMA, III:9	SS, pf
441	Liebes Mandel, wo ist's Bandel?	"	STB, db, 2vn
	Sechs Notturni	"	
346	Luci care, luci belle		SSB, 3bas hn
436	Ecco quel fiero istante (Metastasio)		SSB, 3bas hn
437	Mi lagnero tacendo (Metastasio)		SSB, bas hn, 2cl

438	Se lontan ben mio (Metastasio)		SSB, bas hn, 2cl
439	Due pupille amabile		SSB, 3bas hn
549	Piu non si trovano (Metastasio)		SSB, 3bas hn

MUSGRAVE, THEA (1928-   )
        Primavera   Chester   S, fl

MYROW, FREDERIC (1939-   )
        Songs from the Japanese   Mills Music   S, bcl, db, fl, perc, pf(cel), va, vc, vn

NAYLOR, BERNARD (1907-   )
        The House of Clay   Novello   Bar, bn, cl, fl, va, vc, vn
        * cantata

        Not so Far as the Forest   "   S, st qt

        Sing, O My Love   "   Bar, st
        * cantata

NIELSEN, RICCARDO (1908-   )
        Ganymed (It)   Bongiovanni   S, cl, pf, vc

NIN, JOAQUIN (1879-1949)
        Le Chant du Veilleur   Eschig   Ms, pf, vn

NIN-CULMELL, JOAQUIN MARIA (1908-   )
        Dos poemas de Jorge Manrique   Eschig, 1961   S, st qt
        * 2'30"

NOBRE, MARLOS (1939-   )
  17   Ukrinmakrinkrin   Southern Peer   S, hn, ob, pic

NOVAK, JAN (1921-   )
        Passer Catulli   Modern   Bar, bn, cl, db, fl, hn, ob, va, vc, vn

NOWAK, LIONEL (1911-   0
        Maiden's Song (Hopkins)   ACA   S, cl, pf, vn

        5 Songs (Nemerov)   "   Ms, pf, vc

NYSTEDT, KNUT (1915-   )
  52   The Moment   AMP   S, cel, perc

OBOUSSIER, ROBERT (1900-1957)
    3 Arien nach Klopstock   Bärenreiter   colS, hpd, ob

OGDON, WILL (1921-   )
    By the Isar   APNM   S, afl, db

    Images, a Winter's Calendar   "   S, cl, fl, pf,
                                                     tpt(ob)

    Images of Spring and Summer   "   S, st qt

O'LEARY, JANE
    I Sing the Wind Around   APNM   S, cl, fl

    Poem for a Three Year Old   "   S, cl, fl

    The Prisoner   "   Bar, hn, pf

    Three Voices: Lightning,   "   S, ob, pf
      Peace, Grass

OLIVE, JOSEPH (1941-   )
    Mar-ri-ia-a   ACA   S, cl, fl, hn,
                                               2perc, tp, vc, vn

OLIVER, HAROLD (1942-   )
    Full Fathom Five   APNM   S, cl/bas hn,
                                               cl/bcl, fl/afl/pic,
                                               pf, vn/va

ORBON, JULIAN (1925-   )
    3 Cantigas del Rey   Colombo   S, hpd, 2perc, st qt

ORLAND, HENRY (1918-   )
    Love and Pity   Seesaw   S, cl, va

ORR, BUXTON (1924-   )
    Many Kinds of Yes (cummings)   Eulenburg   SA, pf

ORTHEL, LEON (1905-   )
64   4 Songs   Donemus   S(T), cl, pf

OSTERC, SLAVKO (1895-1941)
    4 Gradnik Lieder   Breitkopf   Ms, st qt

PABLO, LUIS DE (1930-   )
    Commentarios   Modern   S, db, pic, vib

    Glosa   Tonos   S, 2hn, pf, vib

Ein Wort	Tonos	medV, cl, pf, vn

PARKER, ALICE (1925–   )
  Songs for Eve (MacLeish)   Hinshaw   SATB, st qt
  * 75'

PARRIS, ROBERT (1924–   )
  Dreams   APNM   S, cel, db, fl, ob,
                                                       perc, pf, vc

  3 Passacaglias   ACA   S, hpd, vc, vn

PASATIERI, THOMAS (1945–   )
  Far from Love (Dickinson)   Belwin   S, cl, pf, vc, vn

  Heloise and Abelard   Belwin, 1973   SB, pf

  Rites de Passage (Phillips)   Belwin   S(Ms), st qt

PENDERECKI, KRZYSZTOF (1933–   )
  Ecloga VIII (Virgil)   Schott, 1974   CtCtTBarBarB

  Strophes   PWM, 1960   S, spkr, db, fl,
  * 8'   db, perc, pf, va,
                                                       vn, xylorimba

PENN, WIILLIAM (1943–   )
  3 Songs on Teton Sioux Poems   Seesaw   S, 2perc, 2pf

PENNISI, FRANCESCO (1934–   )
  Fossile   Zerboni   mV, bcl, cel, cl,
  * 10'   fl, hn, hpd, 2perc,
                                                       va

PERERA, RONALD C. (1941–   )
  3 Poems of Günter Grass   EC Schirmer   Ms, cl, fl, pf, tp,
                                                       va, vc, vn

PERGOLESI, GIOVANNI BATTISTA (1710–1736)
  Orfeo   Arno, 1968   S, bc, va, 2vn

PERRY, JULIA (1924–1979)
  Stabat mater   Southern, 1954   A, st qt

PERTI, GIACOMO ANTONIO (1661–1756)
  Laudate Pueri   Penn State, 1966   medV, bc, va, vn

PETRASSI, GOFFREDO (1904-   )
        Beatitudines   Zerboni, 1969   B, cl, db, hn,
                                                             timp, va

        Propos d'Alain (E.A. Chartier) Zerboni, 1962   Bar, cl, eng hn,
                                                             mar, perc, timp,
                                                             trbn, 2va, 2vc, xyl

PETYREK, FELIX (1892-1951)
        Late   Universal   V, pf, vn

PEYTON, MALCOLM (1932-   )
        Four Songs from Shakespeare   Mobart, 1982   Ms, 2cl, va, vc, vn
        1 Music to Hear
        2 Orpheus with his Lute
        3 Blow, blow, thou Winter Wind
        4 Lo, in the Orient
        * 9'

        Songs from Walt Whitman   APNM, 1981
        5 Warble for Lilac Time   S, pf, vn
        * first 4 songs for V, pf

        Sonnets from John Donne   Mobart   B, db, hn, trbn,
                                                             va, vc

PINKHAM, DANIEL (1923-   )
        Eight poems of Gerard Manley   Ione, 1970   Bar, va
          Hopkins
        * 15'

        Songs of Innocence (Blake)   EC Schirmer   S, fl, pf

        Time of Times (Norma Farber)   EC Schirmer, 1980   SATB, pf
        1 Ongoing
        2 Long Lullabye
        3 A Quiet Gospel
        4 The Tree in the River
        5 A Cage of Half-light
        6 In the Counting-house
        7 Time of Aster
        * 12'

        Two motets   Ione, 1971   S(T), fl, gtr

PISK, PAUL (1893-   )
    23b The Waning Moon   ACA   S, pf, vc, vn

    37a Meadow Saffrons   New Mus Ed   A, bcl, cl

         5 Folksongs   ACA   medV, 2bn, 2cl, fl,
                                                             2hn, ob, perc, st

PIZZETTI, ILDEBRANDO (1880-1968)
    Tre Canzoni   Ricordi, 1953   hiV, st qt
    1 Donna Lombarda
    2 La Prigioniera
    3 La Pesca dell'anello

PLANTE, DANIEL
    Love in the Asylum   APNM   S, cel, cem, fl/afl,
                                              3hp, ob d'am, perc,
                                            2va, vc

    Two Songs   "   Bar, afl(cl),
                                              gtr(hp), lute

PLESKOW, RAOUL (1931-   )
    2 Bicinia (Lat)   ACA   SS, cl, fl, vc

    For Five Players and Baritone "   Bar, cl, fl, pf,
                                            vc, vn

    Motet and Madrigal   "   ST, cl, fl, pf, vc,
                                              vn

    Three Songs (ancient writings) "   T, bcl, cl, pf, va,
                                            vc, vn

POLLOCK, ROBERT (1946-   )
    Chamber Settings for Baritone Mobart   Bar, bn, cl, ob,
      and 6 Instruments   va, vc, vn

    The Descent (Williams)   "   S, fl, pf

    Song for Soprano (cummings)   "   S, cl, fl

    Tumbling Hair (cummings)   "   A, afl, bcl, pf

POPE, CONRAD
    Wanderers Nachtlied   APNM   S, cl, pf

PORTER, QUINCY (1897-1966)
    12 Songs for Helen and One   ACA   S, bn, cl, fl, ob,
      for Bill   perc, st

POULENC, FRANCIS (1899-1963)
    Le bal masqué (Jacob)   Salabert   Bar(Ms), bn, cl, ob,
                                            perc, pf, va, vn

    Le bestiaire (Apollinaire)   Eschig   V, bn, cl, fl, st qt

    Cocardes (Cocteau)   "   V, cor, perc, trbn,
                                            vn

    Colloque (P. Valery)   Salabert, 1978   SBar, pf

Rhapsodie nègre	Chester, 1919	Bar, Cl, fl, pf, st qt
Un soir de neige (Eluard)	Salabert, 1974	SSATBB

POUSSEUR, HENRI (1929-   )

3 Chants Sacrés (Lat) * 5'	Zerboni	S, va, vc, vn
Echos II de Votre Faust	Universal	Ms, fl, pf, vc

POWELL, MEL (1923-   )

Two Prayer Settings (Goodman, Gregory)	G Schirmer	T, ob, va, vc, vn

PROKOFIEV, SERGEY (1891-1953)

106	Two Russian Duets 1 Vsia koi na svietie to zhienitsia 2 Moskovskaia slavna put'dor ozhka	CW, 17	TB, pf

PURCELL, HENRY (1659-1695)

Sacred works:

Awake, ye dead	PS, 30	BB, bc
Close thine eyes and sleep secure	"	SB, bc
In guilty night	PS, 32	SCt(T)B, bc

Secular duets:

Above the tumults of a busy state	PS, 22	SB, bc
A grasshopper and a fly	PS, 25	SB, bc
Alas, how barbarous are we	PS, 22	SB, bc
A poor blind woman	"	SSB, bc
Come, dear companions of th'Arcadian fields	"	SB, bc
Dulcibella, when e'er I sue for a kiss	"	SB, bc
Fair Cloe, my breast so alarms	"	SB, bc
Fill the bowl with rosy wine	"	SB, bc
Go, tell Amynta, gentle swain	"	SB, bc
Hark, Damon hark	PS, 27	SSB, bc, 2rec, 2vn
Hark how the wild musicians sing	"	TTB, bc, 2vn
Haste, gentle Charon	PS, 22	BB, bc
Has yet your breast no pity learn'd?	"	SB, bc
Hence, fond deceiver	"	SB, bc
Here's to thee, Dick	"	SB, bc
How great are the blessings	"	SB, bc
How pleasant is this flowery plain	"	ST, bc, 2rec

How sweet is the air and refreshing	PS, 22	SB, bc
I saw fair Cloris all alone	"	SB, bc
If ever I more riches did desire	PS, 27	SSTB, bc, 2vn
In a deep vision's intellectual scene	PS, 22	SSB, bc
In all our Cynthia's shining sphere	"	SB, bc
In some kind dream	"	SB, bc
I spy Celia, Celia eyes me	"	SB, bc
Julia, your unjust disdain	"	SB, bc
Let Hector, Achilles and each brave commander	"	SB, bc
Lost is my quiet for ever	"	SB, bc
Nestor, who did to thrice man's age attain	"	SB, bc
O dive custos (Elegy upon the death of Queen Mary)	"	SS, bc
Oft am I by the women told	"	SB, bc
Oh! what a scene does entertain my sight	"	SB, bc, rec(vn)
Saccharissa's grown old	"	SB, bc
See where she sits	"	SB, bc, 2vn
Sit down, my dear Sylvia	"	SB, bc
Sweet tyranness, I now resign	"	SSB, bc
Sylvia, thou brighter eye of night	"	SB, bc
Sylvia, 'tis true you're fair	"	SB, bc
There ne'er was so wretched a lover as I	"	SB, bc
Though my mistress be fair	"	SB, bc
'Tis wine was made to rule the day	"	SSSB, bc
Trip it, trip it in a ring	"	SB, bc
Underneath this myrtle shade	"	SB, bc
We reap all the pleasures	PS, 27	STB, bc, 2rec
Were I to choose the greatest bliss	PS, 22	SB, bc
What can we poor females do?	"	SB, bc
When gay Philander left the plain	"	SB, bc
When, lovely Phyllis, thou art kind	"	SB, bc
When Myra sings	"	SB, bc
When Teucer from his father fled	"	SB, bc
When the cock begins to crow	"	SSB, bc
While bolts and bars my day control	"	SB, bc
While you for me alone had charms	"	SB, bc
Why, my Daphne, why complaining?	"	SB, bc

RAMEAU, JEAN-PHILIPPE (1683-1764)

Cantatas:	OC, iii	
Les amants trahis		SB, bc, gam

Aquilon et Orinthie		B, bc, vn
Le berger fidèle		T, bc, 2vn
L'impatience		S, bc, gam
Orphée		S, bc, gam, vn
Thétis		B, bc, vn

RANDALL, J.K. (1929-   )
Improvisation on a Poem by e.e. cummings	ACA	S(A), asax, cl, gtr, pf, tpt

RAPHAEL, GUNTHER (1903-1960)
69	Palmstrom-Sonate	Breitkopf	T, cl, drums, perc, pf, vn
86	My dark Hands (L. Hughes)	Gerig	Bar, db, drums, pf

RAUSCH, CARLOS
Three Songs from Long Island	APNM	S, hn, tpt, trbn

RAVEL, MAURICE (1895-1937)
Chansons madécasses (de Parny) 1 Nahandove 2 Aous 3 Il est doux...	Durand, 1926	Ms(S), fl, pf, vc
Trois poèmes de Stephane Mallarmé 1 Soupir 2 Placet futile 3 Surgi de la croupe et du bond	Durand, 1914	Ms(S), 2cl, 2fl, pf, st qt

RAWSTHORNE, ALAN (1905-1971)
Tankas of the Four Seasons	Oxford	T, bn, cl, ob, vc, vn

RAXACH, ENRIQUE (1932-   )
Fragmento II (V. Huidobro)	Donemus	S, fl/pic, 2perc
Paraphrase for Alto Voice and Eleven Players	Peters	A, bcl, bn, fl, hn, hp, 2perc, tpt, va, vc, vn

RAZZI, FAUSTO (1932-   )
Improvvisazione III	Zerboni	SSB, db, fl, hpd, 2perc

READ, GARDNER (1913-   )
84b	Two Songs for Voice and Woodwind Quintet	J Fischer	V, ww qnt

REALE, PAUL V. (1943-   )
        Pange Lingua (sacred)   ACA   Bar, cl, 2eng hn,
                                                                 2ob, vc

        The Traveler   "   T, fl, pf

        3 Songs from the Chinese   "   Ms, ob(eng hn),
                                                                  timp, xyl

REDEL, MARTIN CHRISTOPH (1947-   )
        Epilog (Gryphius)   Bote   B, fl, gtr

REGER, MAX (1873-1916)
  6   Drei Chöre   R, 30   SATB, pf
        1 Trost (A. Müller)
        2 Zur Nacht (Fr. Engel)
        3 Abendlied (N. Lenau)

 14   Fünf Duette   Schott   SA, pf
        1 Nachts (Eichendorff)
        2 Abendlied (Goethe)
        3 Sommernacht (D. Saul)
        4 Gäb's ein einzig Brünnelein
        5 O frage nicht! (R. Nawrocki)

111a   Drei Duette   Universal   SA, pf
        1 Waldesstille (L. Rafael)
        2 Frühlingsfeier (U. Steindorff)
        3 Abendgang (M. Brantl)

REICHARD, JOHANN GEORG (1710-1782)
        Weihnachts-Weissagung (Ger/Eng) Deutscher   medV, bc, va, 2vn

REIF, PAUL (1910-1978)
        The Artist   Seesaw   ABar, bn, cl, fl,
                                                            hn, perc, tpt, vn

        Curse of Mauvais Air   "   SATB, pf

        Encounters   "   S, cl

REIMANN, ARIBERT (1936-   )
        Epitaph   Ars Viva   T, 7inst

        3 Spanische Lieder (Sp/Ger)   Bote   S, fl, hp, vc

REISE, JAY (1950-   )
        Alice at the End   APNM   S, cl, ob, perc,
                                                             pf, vn

RESPIGHI, OTTORINO (1879-1936)
        Il Tramonto (Shelley)   Ricordi, 1955   Ms, st qt

RETZEL, FRANK (1948-   )
      Amber Glass   APNM   V, afl, bcl/acl,
      * 21'   pf, vn

      One   "   hiS, hpd, va

REUTTER, HERMANN (1900-   )
22   Misse Brevis   Schott   A, vc, vn

45   Solo-Kantate   "   A, pf, va

57   5 Antique Odes (Sappho)   "   fV, pf, va

73   6 Poems from Goethe's   "   SBar, pf
        "Westöstliches Divan"

      Ein kleines Requiem   "   B, pf, vc

      Kleines geistliches Konzert   "   A, va

      Lyrisches Konzert   "   S, fl, pf, timp

      3 Nocturnes (Nietzche)   Universal   mV, pf, ww

REVUELTAS, SILVESTRE (1899-1940)
      Duo para Pato y Canario   Southern   S, bn, cl, 2fl, ob,
                                 tpt, trbn

REYNOLDS, ROGER (1934-   )
      Again   Peters   SS, 2db, 2fl, 2perc,
                                   tp, 2trbn

      The Emperor of Ice Cream (W.   "   8V, db, perc, pf
        Stevens)
        * 14'

RHODES, PHILLIP (1940-   )
      Autumn Setting   "   S, st qt

RICE, THOMAS (1933-   )
      Fully Clothed in Armor   Seesaw   SB, vc, vn

RIEGGER, WALLINGFORD (1885-1961)
      Music for Voice and Flute   Bomart, 1950   hiV, fl

RILEY, DENNIS (1943-   )
8   Cantata I (Lawrence)   Peters   Ms, pf, sax, vc, vib

      5 Songs on Japanese Haiku   "   S, cl, vc, vn

RIMSKY-KORSAKOV, NIKOLAY ANDREYEVICH (1844-1908)
  47   Two duets   Belwin, 1980   MsBar(ST), pf
            1 Pan (Maykov)
            2 Pesnya pesen (Mey)

  52   Two duets   RK, 46a
            1 Gornîy kluch   SMs(TBar), pf
            2 Angel i demon   SBar(TMs), pf

  53   Strekozî (Tolstoy)   "   SSA, pf

ROCCA, LODOVICO (1895-   )
            Biribu Occhi di Rana (N.   Carisch   Ms(Bar), st qt
              Davicini)

ROCHBERG, GEORGE (1918-   )
            String Quartet #2   Presser   S, st qt

            Blake Songs   Leeds, 1963   S, bcl, cel, cl,
                                                            fl, hp, va, vc, vn

ROCKMAKER, JODY
            Two Songs   APNM   T, va

RODRIGO, JOAQUIN (1901-   )
            2 Poemas (J.R. Jiménez)   UME   Ms, fl

RONNEFELD, PETER (1935-1965)
            2 Lieder zur Pauke   Modern   A, fl, 4timp

            4 Wiegenlieder   "   S, fl

RONSHEIM, JOHN RICHARD (1927-   )
            Sailing Homeward   APNM   S, vib

            Two Settings of George Herbert   "   S, vib

            Words from Shakespeare   "   S, hp, pf, vib
            * 6'

ROREM, NED (1923-   )
            Ariel (Sylvia Plath)   Boosey, 1974   S, cl, pf
            1 Words
            2 Poppies in July
            3 The Hanging Man
            4 Poppies in October
            5 Lady Lazarus

Four Dialogues (Frank O'Hara)   Boosey   MsT, 2pf

Gloria   Boosey, 1972   SMs, pf

King Midas (Howard Moss)   Boosey   ST, pf

Last Poems of Wallace Stevens   "   S, pf, vc

Mourning Scene from Samuel   "   T, st qt

Serenade on Five English Poems Boosey, 1978   medV, pf, va, vn

ROSALES, ANTONIO (ca. 1740-1801)
    El Recitado   UME   STT, pf

ROSENMULLER, JOHANN (ca. 1619-1684)
    Danket dem Herrn   Hänssler   AT, bc, 2vn
                                (Die Kantate, 41)

    Das ist ein köstliche Ding Hänssler   ST, bc, 2va, 2vn
                                (Die Kantate, 44)

    Das ist meine Freude   Hänssler   S, bc, 2vn

    Ecce nunc benedicite   Nagel, 1932   lowV, bc, 2vn

    Hebet eure Augen auf   Hänssler, 1960   ST, bc, 2vn
                                (Die Kantate, 38)

    Herr, mein Gott, ich danke Dir Hänssler, 1963 TTB, bc, 2vn
                                (Die Kantate, 164)

    Ich bin das Brot des Lebens Hänssler, 1963   ATB, bc, 2vn
                                (Die Kantate, 163)

    In hac misera valle   Kistner   SSB, bc
                                (Organum, 24)

    Lieber Herre Gott   Bärenreiter, 1964 S, bc, 2gam
    * Advent

    Meine Seele harret auf Gott Hänssler, 1960   ATB, bc, 2vn
                                (Die Kantate, 40)

    Siehe, des Herren Auge   Hänssler, 1963   STB, bc, 2vn
                                (Die Kantate, 162)

    Weil wir wissen dass der Mensch Hanssler, 1963 ATB, bc, 2vn
                                (Die Kantate, 161)

ROSSI, SALAMONE (ca. 1570-1630)
    Il Primo Libro delle   Israeli   3V, bc
        Canzonette (It/Heb)

ROSSINI, GIOACHINO (1792-1868)
        L'asia in Faville   Boosey (HL)   SATB, pf

        Péchés de Vieillesse
            Aurora   Sov Mus, 1955,   ATB, pf
                                       no 8
            Duetto buffo di due gatti   QR, iv, and   2V, pf
                                       Ricordi
            I Gondolieri   QR, vii   SATB, pf
            La Passeggiata   "   SATB, pf
            Le départ des promis (Pacini) Houghton   SA, pf
            Les amants de Seville   QR, v   AT, pf
            Soupirs et sourires (G.   Houghton   ST, pf
              Torre)
            Toast pour le nouvel an   QR, vii   SATB, pf

        Les soirées musicales   Ricordi
          9 La regate veneziana (Pepoli)   SS, pf
        10 La pesca (Metastasio)   SS, pf
        11 La serenata (Pepoli)   ST, pf
        12 La marinari (Pepoli)   TB, pf
        * Nos 1-8 for V, pf

ROUSE, CHRISTOPHER (1949-   )
        The Kiss   ACA   Bar, bcl, cel, hp,
                                                    perc, pf

ROUSSEL, ALBERT (1869-1937)
        Deux poèmes de Ronsard   Durand, 1924   hiV, fl
        1 Rossignol, mon mignon...
        2 Ciel, aer et vens...

ROVICS, HOWARD (1936-   )
        Echo   ACA   medV, fl, pf

        Haunted Objects   ACA, 1974   S, nar(m), bn, eng
                                                      hn(ob), hecklephone
                                                   (eng hn), ob, tp

        The Hunter   ACA   S, va

RUBENSTEIN, ANTON (1829-1894)
48   Duets   Peters   SA, pf
        1 Der Engel (Lermontof)
        2 Sang das Vögelein (Delwig)
        3 Im Heimischen Land
          (Aleksjeff)
        4 Volkslied ("Mägdlein auf
          die Wiese gingen")
        5 Wanders Nachtlied (after
          Goethe)
        6 Beim Scheiden
        7 Die Nacht (Jukowsky)
        8 Die Wolke (Pushkin)
        9 Das Vöglein (Pushkin)

        10 Die Turteltaube und der
           Wanderer (Dmitrief)
        11 Am Abend (Dawidoff)
        12 Volkslied (Kolzoff)

    67   Duets   Peters   SA, pf
        1 Lied der Vögelein (Schultze)
        2 Waldlied (Lenau)
        3 Frühlingsglaube (Uhland)
        4 Vorüber (H. Kletke)
        5 Meeresabend (von Strachwitz)
        6 Lied ("Die Lotosblume") (Heine)

RUDD-MOORE, DOROTHY (1940-   )
        From the Dark Tower   ACA   Ms, pf, vc

        12 Quatrains from the Rubaiyat   "   Ms, ob

        Sonnets on Love, Rosebuds and   "   S, vn
           Death

        Weary Blues   "   B, vc

RUYNEMAN, DANIEL (1886-1963)
        Reflexions I   Donemus   S, fl, gtr, perc,
                                                         va, vib, xyl

        Sous le pont Mirabeau   "   SA, fl, hp, st qt

SAINT-SAENS, CAMILLE (1835-1921)
        Le bonheur est chose légère   Choudens   hiV, pf, vn
           (Barbier)

        El desdichado (Barbier)   Durand, Vingt   SS, pf
                                      mélodies (NYPL)

        Une flûte invisible   Durand   V, fl, pf

        Pastorale   Durand, Vingt   SBar, pf
                                      mélodies (NYPL)

        Romance du soir (Croze)   NYPL   SATB

        Viens (Hugo)   Durand, Vingt   SBar, pf
                                      mélodies (NYPL)

        Violons dans le soir   Durand   Ms(Bar), vn

SALMON, KAREL (1897-1974)
        Elegy and Dance   Israeli   S, 2fl(vn)

SALVIUCCI, GIOVANNI (1907-1937)
        Salmo di David   Carisch   S, bn, cl, fl, hn,
                                                          ob, pf, tpt, trbn

SALZMAN, ERIC (1933-   )
     In Praise of the Owl and the   MCA   S, cl, fl, gtr, va,
        Cuckoo (Shakespeare)   vn

SANDSTROM, SVEN-DAVID (1942-   )
     Just a Bit   Nordiska   S, bn, hp, vn

SAPIEYEVSKI, JERZY (1945-   )
     Love Songs (Lindbergh)   Mercury   S, fl, perc, st qt

SARGON, SIMON
     Patterns in Blue   Boosey, 1976   medV, cl, pf

SAUGUET, HENRI (1901-   )
     Trois chants de contemplation   Leduc, 1975   AB, qt(fl, br,
     * 9'30"   ww)(pf)

SAVIONI, MARIO (1608-1685)
     6 Cantatas   Presser   1-3V, bc

SCARLATTI, ALESSANDRO (1660-1725)
     Ardo e ver per d'amore   Kunzelmann   S, bc, fl

     Arianna   Peters, 1970   S, bc, 2vn

     Bella madre de'fiori   CEN, <u>Due Cantate</u>, S, bc, 2vn
                                 1969 <u>(HL)</u>

     Cantata pastorale per la   Oxford, 1969   S, hpd, st qt
        nascita di Nostro Signore

     Correa nel seno amato   Bärenreiter, 1974 S, bc, 2vn

     Infirmata vulnerate   Bieler, 1959 (<u>Die</u> A, bc, 2vn
                                 <u>Kantate</u>, 5)

     Nacqui a' sospiri e al pianto CEN, <u>Due Cantate</u>, S, bc, 2vn
                                 1969 <u>(HL)</u>

     Solitudine avvenne   Zimmermann   S, bc, fl

     Su le sponde del Tebro   Müller, 1956   S, bc, tpt, 2vn

SCARLATTI, DOMENICO (1685-1757)
     Salve Regina   Bärenreiter, 1971 SA, bc(org)

SCHAFER, R. MURRAY (1933-   )
     Arcana   Berandol   medV, cl, fl/pic,
     * 16'   hp, perc, pf, tpt,
                                            trbn, vc, vn

Minnelieder	Berandol	Ms, ww qnt
Requiems for the Party Girl	"	Ms, cl/bcl, fl/pic, hn, hp, perc, pf, st tr
5 Studies on Texts by Prudentius	"	S, 4fl

SCHAT, PETER (1935–   )

Canto General	Donemus	S, pf, vn
Entelechie II	"	S, cel, cl, fl, hp, perc, pf, tpt, va, vc, vib, vn
Improvisaties uit Het Labyrint	"	ATB, bcl, db, perc, pf

SCHEIN, JOHANN HERMANN (1586–1630)

Israelsbrünnlein	A, l	SSATB, bc

   Ach Herr, ach meiner schöne
   Da Jakob vollendet hatte
   Dennoch bleibe ich stets an
     dir
   Die mit Tränen säen
   Drei schöne Ding sind
   Freue dich des Weibes deiner
     Jugend
   Der Herr denket an uns
   Herr, lass meine Klage
   Ich bin die Wurzel des
     Geschlechtes David
   Ich bin jung gewesen
   Ich freue mich im Herren
   Ich lasse dich nicht
   Ihr Heiligen, lobsinget dem
     Herren
   Ist nicht Ephraim mein teurer
     Sohn
   Lehre uns bedenken
   Lieblich und schöne sein ist
     nichts
   Nun danket alle Gott
   O Herr, ich bin dein Knecht
   O, Herr Jesu Christe
   Siehe an die Werk Gottes
   Siehe, nach Trost war mir
     sehr bange
   Unser Leben währet siebnzig
     Jahr
   Was betrübst du dich, meine
     Seele
   Wem ein tugendsam Weib
     bescheret ist
   Wende dich, Herr, und sei mir
     gnädig

Zion spricht: Der Herr hat
mich verlassen

Opella novella   A, 4

Ach Gott vom Himmel sieh   SS, bc
darein

An Wasserflüssen Babylon   SS, bc

Aus tiefer Not schrei ich zu   SS, bc
dir

Christ lag in Todesbanden   SST, bc

Christ, unser Herr, zum   SS, alto inst, bc,
Jordan kam   tenor inst

Christe, der du bist Tag und   SS, bc
Licht

Da Jesus an dem Kreuze stand   SS, bc

Dies sind die heiligen zehen   SS, bc
Gebot

Durch Adams Fall ist ganz   SS, bc
verderbt

Ein feste Burg ist unser Gott   SS, bc

Erbarm dich mein, O Herre   SS, bc
Gott

Es ist das Heil uns kommen   SS, bc
her

Es spricht der Unweisen Mund   SS, bc
wohl

Gelobet seist du, Jesu Christ   SST, bc

Gott der Vater wohn uns bei   SS, bc

Herr Christ, der einig Gottes   SS, bc
Sohn

Herr Gott, dich loben alle wir   SS, bc

Ich ruf zu dir, Herr Jesu   SS, bc
Christ

Komm, heiliger Geist, Herre   SST, bc
Gott

Mit Fried und Freud ich fahr   SS, bc
dahin

Mitten wir im Loben sind   SS, bc

Nun freut euch, Lieben   SS, bc
Christen gmein

Nun komm, der Heiden Heiland   SST, bc

Nun lob, mein Seel, den   SS, bc
Herren

O Jesu Christe, Gottes Sohn   S, bc, vn

O Lamm Gottes unschüldig   SS, bc

Vater unser im Himmelreich   SS, bc

Vom Himmel hoch da komm ich   SST, bc
her

Wo Gott der Herr nicht bei   SS, bc
uns halt

Wo Gott zum Haus nicht gibt   SS, bc
sein Gunst

Studentenschmaus (1626)   A, 6   SSATB, bc

Frischauf, ihr Klosterbrüder
mein

Holla, gut Gsell

Ihr Brüder, lieben Brüder
mein

      Sieh da, sieh da, ihr lieben
        Herrn
      So da, mein liebes Brüderlein

Diletti Pastorali Hirtenlust	A, 8	SSATB, bc
All wilden Tier im grünen Wald		
Als Filli schön und fromm		
Amor, das liebe Räuberlein		
Aurora schön mit ihrem Haar		
Cupido blind, das Venuskind		
In Filli schönen Augelein		
Mein Schifflein lief im wilden Meer		
Mirtillo hat ein Schäfelein		
O Amarilli zart		
O Amarilli, schönste Zier		
O Venus und Cupido blind		
Unlängst dem blinden Gottelein		
Die Vögelein singen		
Wenn Filli ihre Liebesstrahl		
Wie kömmt's, o zarte Filli mein		

SCHELLE, JOHANN (1648-1701)

	Ach, mein herzliebes Jesulein	Breitkopf	2V, bc

SCHMITT, FLORENT (1870-1958)

99	3 Trios	Durand	SMsA, pf
116	Trois liturgies joyeuses	Durand, 1951	SATB, org
	1 Veni Creator		
	2 Adjiciat Dominus		
	3 Magnificat		
136	3 Duos	Durand	hiVmedV, pf
	4 Monocantes	"	hiV, fl, hp, va, vc, vn

SCHOECK, OTHMAR (1886-1957)

42	Wanderspruche	Breitkopf	T(S), cl, hn, perc, pf
47	Notturno	Universal	Bar, st qt

SCHOENBERG, ARNOLD (1874-1951)

10	String quartet No. 2	Universal, 1925	S, st qt
	Herzgewächse (Maeterlinck)	Universal, 1947	hiS, cel, harm, hp
	Nachtwandler (G. Falke)	Belmont, 1969	V, pf, pic, sn drum, tpt

Ode to Napoleon (Byron)	Belmont, 1973	spkr, pf, st qt
Pierrot lunaire	Universal, 1941	spkr, cl/bcl, fl/pic, pf, vc, vn/va
Serenade	Hansen, 1924	Bar, bcl, cl, gtr, mand, va, vc, vn

SCHOLLUM, ROBERT (1913-   )

49	Ein Jeder von dem Seinen (A. Silesius)	Doblinger	S, pf, vn
	3 Weihnachtsgesänge	"	fV, st tr

SCHONBACH, DIETER (1931-   )

Canticum Psalmi Resurrectiones	Universal	S, 2fl, gtr, perc, tpt, 2va
Lyric Songs	Peters	Ms, 2pf

SCHRAMM, HAROLD (1935-1971)

Song of Taynmanavar	New Mus Ed	S, fl

SCHUBERT, FRANZ (1797-1828)

D			
	Mixed voices:		
168	Begräbnislied (F. Klopstock)	NSA, xii	SATB, pf
168a	Osterlied (Klopstock)	"	SATB, pf
232	Hymne an den Unendlichen (Schiller)	"	SATB, pf
439	An die Sonne (J.P. Uz)	"	SATB, pf
609	Lebenslust (J.K. Unger)	"	SATB, pf
666	Kantate zum Geburtstag des Sängers Johann Michae	"	STB, pf
763	Des Tages Weihe	"	SATB, pf
815	Gebet (Fouque)	"	SATB, pf
826	Der Tanz (Schnitzer)	"	SATB, pf
930	Der Hochzeitsbraten (Schober)	"	STB, pf
985	Gott im Ungewitter (Uz)	"	SATB, pf
986	Gott der Weltschöpfer (Uz)	"	SATB, pf
352	Licht und Liebe (M. von Collin)	NSA, xiv	ST, pf
877	Gesänge aus Wilhelm Meister		
	1 Mignon und der Harfner	NSA, xvi	ST, pf
	Male voices (major works):	NSA, xii	
37	Die Advokaten (Baron Engelhart)		TTB, pf
80	Zur Namensfeier meines Vaters (F. Schubert)		TTB, gtr
140	Klage um Ali Bey (M. Claudius)		TTB, pf
267	Trinklied		TTBB, pf

268	Bergknappenlied		TTBB, pf
441	Cantate zur 50 jahrigen Jubelfeier Salieri's		TTB, pf
513	La pastorella		TTBB, pf
714	Gesang der Geister über den Wassern (Goethe)		TTTTBBBB, db, 2va, 2vc
598	Das Dörfchen (Burger)		TTBB, gtr(pf)
710	Im Gegenwärtigen Vergangenes (Goethe)		TTBB, pf
724	Die Nachtigall (Unger)		TTBB, gtr(pf)
740	Frühlingsgesang (Schober)		TTBB, gtr(pf)
747	Geist der Liebe (Matthisson)		TTBB, gtr(pf)
809	Gondelfahrer (Mayhofer)		TTBB, pf
835	Bootgesang (Scott, tran Storck)		TTBB, pf
	Female voices (major works):	NSA, xii	
269	Das Leben (Wannovius)		SSA, pf
706	Der 23. Psalm (tr. M. Mendelssohn)		SSAA, pf
757	Gott in der Natur (von Kleist)		SSAA, pf
836	Coronach (Scott, tr. Storck)		SSA, pf
	Songs:		
943	Auf dem Strom (Rellstab)	Kalmus, others	S(T), hn(vc), pf
965	Der Hirt auf dem Felsen (Müller)	Lienau, Peters, G Schirmer	S, cl, pf

SCHULLER, GUNTHER (1925-   )
6 Renaissance Lyrics

AMP, 1979   T, db, fl, ob, pf, va, vc, vn

SCHUMAN, WILLIAM (1910-   )
In Sweet Music (Shakespeare)   Presser   V, fl, hp, va

SCHUMANN, ROBERT (1810-1856)

29	Drei Gedichte (Geibel)	SW, x/2	
	1 Ländliches Lied		SS, pf
	2 Lied		SSS, pf
	3 Zigeunerleben		SATB, pf
34	Vier Duette	Peters	ST, pf
	1 Liebesgarten (Reinick)		
	2 Liebhabers Ständchen (Burns)		
	3 Unterm Fenster (Burns)		
	4 Familien-Gemälde (A. Grun)		
37	Zwölf Gedichte (Rückert)	"	ST, pf
	6 Liebste, was kann denn uns scheiden?		ST, pf
	7 Schön ist das Fest des Lenzes		ST, pf
	12 So wahr die Sonne scheinet		ST, pf

43	Drei zweistimmige Lieder	Peters	SA, pf
	1 Wenn ich ein Vöglein wär (Knaben Wunderhorn)		
	2 Herbstlied (S.A. Mahlmann)		
	3 Schön Blümelein (Reinick)		
64	Romanzen und Balladen	SW, xiii/3	
	1 Entflieh mit mir und sei mein Weib		T, pf
	2 Es fiel ein Reif in der Frühlingsnacht		S, pf
	3 Auf ihrem Grab		ST, pf
	* 3 Tragodie (Heine)		
74	Spanisches Liederspiel (Geibel)	Peters	
	1 Erste Begegnung		SA, pf
	2 Intermezzo		TB, pf
	3 Liebesgram		SA, pf
	4 In der Nacht		ST, pf
	5 Es ist verraten		SATB, pf
	6 Melancholie		S, pf
	7 Geständnis		T, pf
	8 Botschaft		SA, pf
	9 Ich bin geliebt		SATB, pf
	10 Der Kontrabandiste		Bar, pf
78	Vier Duette	"	ST, pf
	1 Tanzlied (Ruckert)		
	2 Er und Sie (Kerner)		
	3 Ich denke dein (Goethe)		
	4 Wiegenlied (Hebbel)		
79	Lieder-Album für die Jugend	SW, xiii/3	
	9 Mailied (C.A. Overbeck)		SS, pf
	15 Das Glück (Hebbel)		SS, pf
	18 Frühlingslied (Hoffman von Fallersleben)		SS, pf
	20 Die Schwalben (Des Knaben Wunderhorn)		SS, pf
	24 Spinnelied		3fV, pf
101	Minnespiel (Rückert)	SW, x/2	
	1 Meine Töne still und heiter		T, pf
	2 Liebster, deine Worte stehlen		S, pf
	3 Ich bin dein Baum		AB, pf
	4 Mein schöner Stern!		T, pf
	5 Schön ist das Fest des Lenzes		SATB, pf
	6 O Freund, mein Schirm, mein Schutz!		A(S), pf
	7 Die tausend Grüsse		ST, pf
	8 So wahr die Sonne scheinet		SATB, pf
103	Mädchenlieder (E. Kulman)	Peters	SS(SA), pf
	1 Mailied		
	2 Frühlingslied		
	3 An die Nachtigall		
	4 An den Abendstern		

114	Drei Lieder	SW, x/2	3fV, pf
	1 Nanie		
	2 Triolett		
	3 Spruch		
138	Spanische Liebeslieder (Geibel)	"	
	1 Vorspiel		pf 4hnds
	2 Tief im Herzen trag ich Pein		S, pf 4hnds
	3 O wie lieblich ist das Mädchen		T, pf 4hnds
	4 Bedeckt mich mit Blumen		SA, pf 4hnds
	5 Flutenreicher Ebro		Bar, pf 4hnds
	6 Intermezzo		pf 4hnds
	7 Weh, wie zornig ist das Mädchen		T, pf 4hnds
	8 Hoch, hoch sind die Berge		A, pf 4hnds
	9 Blaue Augen hat das Mädchen		TB, pf 4hnds
	10 Dunkler Lichtglanz		SATB, pf 4hnds
	Duette für zwei Singstimmen	Peters	2V, pf
	* 34 selected duets		
	Sommerruh (C. Schad)	"	2V, pf

SCHUTZ, HEINRICH (1585-1672)

SWV	Kleiner geistlichen Concerten I	N, x-xi	
286	Der Herr ist gross		SS, bc
287	O liebe Herre Gott		SS, bc
288	Ihr heiligen, lobsinget dem Herren		SS, bc
289	Erhöre mich, wenn ich rufe		SS, bc
290	Wohl dem, der nicht wandelt		SA, bc
291	Schaffe in mir, Gott, ein reines Herz		ST, bc
292	Der Herr schauet vom Himmel		SB, bc
293	Lobet den Herren, der zu Zion wohnet		AA, bc
294	Eins bitte ich vom Herren		TT, bc
295	O hilf, Christe, Gottes Sohn		TT, bc
296	Fürchte dich nicht, ich bin mit dir		BB, bc
297	O Herr hilf		SST, bc
298	Das Blut Jesu Christi		SSB, bc
299	Die Gottseligkeit ist zu allen Dingen nutz		SSB, bc
300	Himmel und Erde vergehen		BBB, bc
301	Nun komm, der Heiden Heiland		SSBB, bc
302	Ein Kind ist uns geboren		SATB, bc
303	Wir gläuben all an einen Gott		SSTB, bc
304	Siehe, mein Fürsprecher ist im Himmel		SATB, bc
	Kleiner geistlichen Concerten II	N, x, xi	
311	Habe deine Lust an dem Herren		SS, bc
312	Herr, ich hoffe darauf		SS, bc
313	Bone Jesu, verbum Patris		SS(TT), bc

314	Verbum caro factum est	SS, bc
315	Hodie Christus natus est	ST, bc
316	Wann unsre Augen schlafen ein	SB, bc
317	Meister wir haben die ganze Nacht gearbeitet	TT, bc
318	Die Furcht des Herren	TT, bc
319	Ich beuge meine Knie	BB, bc
320	Ich bin jung gewesen	BB, bc
321	Herr, wann ich nur dich habe	SST, bc
322	Rorate coeli desuper	SSB, bc
323	Joseph, du Sohn David	SSB, bc
324	Ich bin die Auferstehung	TT(SS)B, bc
325	Die Seele Christi heilige mich	ATB, bc
326	Ich ruf zu dir, Herr Jesu Christ	SSSB, bc
327	Allein Gott in der Höh sei Ehr	SSTT, bc
328	Veni, Sancte Spiritus	SSTT, bc
329	Ist Gott für uns	SATB, bc
330	Wer will uns scheiden von der Liebe Gottes	SATB, bc
331	Die Stimm des Herren	SATB, bc
332	Jubilate Deo omnis terra	SATB, bc
335	Was betrübst du dich	SSATB, bc
336	Quemadmodum desiderat cervus	SATTB, bc
337	Aufer immensam, Deus, aufer iram	SATTB, bc
	Symphoniarum sacrarum II N, xv	
341	Mein Herz ist bereit	S(T), bc, 2vn
342	Singet dem Herren ein neues Lied	S(T), bc, 2vn
343	Herr, unser Herrscher	S(T), bc, 2vn
344	Meine Seele erhebt den Herren	S, bc, 2vn
345	Der Herr ist meine Stärke	S(T), bc, 2vn
346	Ich werde nicht sterben	S(T), bc, 2vn
347	Ich danke dir, Herr	S(T), bc, 2vn
348	Herzlich lieb hab ich dich, o Herr	A, bc, 2vn
349	Frohlocket mit Händen	T, bc, 2vn
350	Lobet den Herrn in seinem Heiligtum	T, bc, 2vn
351	Hütet euch, dass eure Herzen	B, bc, 2vn
352	Herr, nun lässest du deinen Diener	B, bc, 2vn
353	Was betrübst du dich	SS(TT), bc, 2vn
354	Verleih uns Frieden genadiglich	SS(TT), bc, 2vn
356	Es steh Gott auf	SS(TT), bc, 2vn
357	Wie ein Rubin in feinem Golde leuchtet	SA, bc, 2vn
359	Der Herr ist mein Licht	TT, bc, 2vn
360	Zweierlei bitte ich, Herr	TT, bc, 2vn
361	Herr, neige deine Himmel	BB, bc, 2vn
362	Von Aufgang der Sonnen	BB, bc, 2vn
363	Lobet den Herrn, alle Heiden	ATB, bc, 2vn
364	Die so ihr den Herren fürchtet	ATB, bc, 2vn
365	Drei schöne Dinge seind	TTB, bc, 2vn
366	Von Gott will ich nicht lassen	SSB, bc, 2vn
367	Freuet euch des Herren	ATB, bc, 2vn

431	Gib unsern Fürsten		SS(TT), bc, 2vn
438	Iss dein Brot mit Freuden		SB, bc, 2vn
	Symphoniarum sacrarum I	N, xiv	
267	Benedicam Dominum in omni tempore		STB, bc, cornetto(vn)
268	Exquisivi Dominum		STB, bc, cornetto(vn)
269	Fili mi, Absalon		B, bc, 2trbn, 2trbn(vn)

SCHWANTNER, JOSEPH (1943-   )

| | Shadows II | ACA | Bar, bcl, cl, fl, gtr, mand, perc, tp, va, vc, vn |

SEIBER, MATYAS (1905-1960)

	Four Hungarian Folksongs 1 Lament 2 Quarrel 3 Farewell 4 Soldier's Song	Augener, 1956	medV, vn
	Four Medieval French Songs 1 Gentilz galans de France 2 Pastourelle 3 A vous amanz 4 Pourquoi me bat mon mari?	Zerboni, 1964	medV, gam(vc), gtr, va d'am(va)
	Drei Morgensternlieder 1 Die Trichter 2 Das Knie 3 Das Nasobem	Universal, 1956	S, cl

SEMEGEN, DARIA (1946-   )

| | Lieder auf der Flucht | ACA | S, cl, fl, hn, 2perc, pf, vib, vc, vn |

SEREBRIER, JOSE (1938-   )

| | Erotica | Southern Peer | S, ww qnt |

SEYFRIT, MICHAEL EUGENE (1947-   )

| | Winter's Warmth | ACA | B, bn, cl, hp, va, vc, vn |

SHAPEY, RALPH (1921-   )

| | Walking Upright Songs (Vera Klement) | Presser | fV, vn |

SHEPHERD, ARTHUR (1880-1958)

| | Tryptych (Tagore) | " | hiV, st qt |

SHIELDS, ALICE (1943-   )
    Wildcat Songs   ACA   S, pic

SHIFRIN, SEYMOUR (1926-1979)
    A Renaissance Garland   Mobart, 1979   ST, gam, lute,
    1 Sonnet (Sir Thomas Wyatt)   perc, rec
    2 Ballad
    3 An excellent Sonnet of a
      Nimph (Sir Phillip Sidney)
    4 Sonnet (Shakespeare)

    Satires of Circumstance (Hardy) Peters   Ms, cl, db, fl, pf,
    * 16'30"   vc, vn

SHOSTAKOVICH, DMITRY (1906-1975)
 79   Gesänge nach Hebräischen   Peters, 1958   SAT, pf
      Volksdichtungen
    1 Klage über den Tod eines   SA, pf
      kleinen Kindes
    2 Die fürsorgliche Mutter zur   SA, pf
      Tante
    3 Wiegenlied   A, pf
    4 Vor einer langen Trennung   ST, pf
    5 Warnung   S, pf
    6 Der verlassene Vater   AT, pf
    7 Wiegenlied von der Not   T, pf
    8 Winter   SAT, pf
    9 Schönes Leben   T, pf
   10 Lied eines Mädchens   S, pf
   11 Das Glück   SAT, pf

127   Romanzen-Suite   Deutscher, 1970   S, pf, vc, vn
    * 7 movements

SIEGL, OTTO (1896-   )
123   Wald-Sonate   Böhm   S, st
    * sacred cantata

    Die Schenke am See   Doblinger   S, 4st

SILSBEE, ANN L. (1930-
    Only the Cold Bare Moon   ACA   S, fl, pf

SILVERMAN, FAYE-ELLEN (1947-   )
    In Shadows   Seesaw   S, cl, gtr

SIMONS, NETTY (1913-   )
    Diverse Settings   Merion   S, bn, fl, cl, db,
                                                       ob, perc, va, vc,
                                                       vib, 2vn

    3 Trialogues (Dylan Thomas)   "   MsBar, va

SIMS, EZRA (1928-   )
  Celebration of Dead Ladies ACA   V, afl, bas hn, cl,
   (J. Stephens)   perc, va, vc
   * microtonal

  3 Haiku   "   Ms, cast, tabla

  In Memoriam Alice Hawthorne "   TBar, spkr, 4cl,
                     2mar

SINGER, JEANNE (1924-   )
  Sonnet (Benton)   AMC   S, cl(va), vn

  To Stir a Dream   "   S, cl

SINOPOLI, GIUSEPPE (1946-   )
  Sunyata   Zerboni   S, st qnt

SMIT, LEO (1900-1943)
  La Mort   Donemus   SA, pf

  4 Motets (Eng)   Broude   medV, 2fl, vn(2srec,
                     treb rec)

SOLER, JOSE (1935-   )
  Passio Jesu Christi   Moeck   SBar, hpd, org, va,
   * Easter   vc

SOURIS, ANDRE (1890-1970)
  Comptines pour Enfants Zerboni   SMs, cl, pf, vn
   Sinistres (F. Marc)

  L'autre Voix (Guiette)   CeBeDeM   S, cl, fl, pf, vc,
                     vn

SPIES, CLAUDIO (1925-   )
  5 Psalms   Boosey   ST, bn, fl, hn,
                     mand, va, vc

SPOHR, LOUIS (1784-1859)
103 Sechs deutsche Lieder Bärenreiter, 1971 S(Ms), cl, pf
  1 Sei still mein Herz
   (Schweitzer)
  2 Zwiegesang (Reinick)
  3 Sehnsucht (Geibel)
  4 Wiegenlied (von Fallersleben)
  5 Das heimliche Lied (Koch)
  6 Wach auf

154 Six Songs for Baritone Bärenreiter   Bar, pf, vn

SREBOTNJAK, ALOJZ (1931-   )
      War Pictures   Drustvo   A, perc, pf

STAEMPFLI, EDWARD (1908-   )
      Tagebuch aus Israel   Israeli   A, cl, vc, vn

STARER, ROBERT (1924-   )
      Cantamus   "   SBar, pf, vn

STEARNS, PETER PINDAR (1931-   )
      3 Love Songs   ACA   S, bcl, cl, hp,
                                                      tpt, trbn, va, va,
                                                      vn

      5 Lyrics (Gibran)   "   S, fl, va

      3 Sacred Songs   "   S, hn, ob, vc

STEDRON, MILOS (1942-   )
      Sic et Non   Czech   TB, ob, pic, trbn,
                                                      tuba

STEFFENS, WALTER (1934-   )
 3b   Neue Gleichnisse   Breitkopf   S, cl, fl, va

 9   Oboe Songs   "   lowV, ob

STEINER, GITTA (1932-   )
      Cantos   Seesaw   medV, vib

      Concert Piece for Seven #2   "   S, db, fl, 2perc, pf

      Concert Piece for Seven #1   "   S, db, fl, 2perc, pf

      Dream Dialogue   "   S, perc

      Interludes   "   S, vib

      Music for Four   "   S, db, 2perc

      New Poems for Voice and   "   medV, vib
        Vibraphone

      3 Poems for Voice and 2   "   medV, 2perc
        Percussion

      Four Songs for Medium Voice   "   medV, vib
        and Vibraphone

      Trio for Voice, Piano and   "   medV, perc, pf
        Percussion

STERNBERG, ERICH WALTER (1891-1974)
         The Distant Flute (Heb/Ger)   Isr Mus Inst   A, fl

         String Quartet #1   Israeli   A, st qt

STEVENS, HALSEY (1908-   )
         3 Japanese Folk Songs   ACA   medV, pf, vc, vn

         2 Shakespeare Songs   "   Ms, cl, fl

STEWART, FRANK GRAHAM (1920-   )
         First Joy of Marriage   Seesaw   S, 2perc

STOCK, DAVID (1939-   )
         Scat (syllables only)   ACA   S, bcl, fl, vc, vn

STOUT, ALAN (1932-   )
  14   Commentary on T'ung Jen   "   S(T), ob, pf, opt
                                                              drums

  36   Landscape   "   Ms, eng hn, fl, hp,
                                                              tam

  37   Christmas Antiphon   "   S(T), org, va, 4tom

  73   3 An Allegory: Pride   "   S, cl, perc, pf, vc

         Canticum Canticorum   Peters   S, bn, cel, cl, fl,
                                                              hn, hp, ob, perc, va

STRAESSER, JOEP (1934-   )
         Ramasasiri   Donemus   Ms, fl, hpd, perc,
                                                              pf

STRAUSS, RICHARD (1864-1949)
         Alphorn (Kerner)   CW, 3   S, hn, pf

STRAVINSKY, IGOR (1882-1971)
         Berceuses du chat   Chester, 1917   A, 3cl
         1 Sur le poele
         2 Interieur
         3 Dodo
         4 Ce qu'il a, le chat

         Elegy for J.F.K.   Boosey, 1964   Ms(Bar), 3cl

         In memoriam Dylan Thomas   Boosey, 1954   T, st qt, 4trbn

         Three Japanese lyrics (Rus/Fr)   Boosey   S, 2cl, 2fl, pf,
         1 Akahito   st qt
         2 Mazatsumi
         3 Tsaraiuki

Pastorale	B Schott, 1962	V, bn, cl, eng hn, ob
Two Poems of Konstantin Bal'mont 1 Nezabudoochka-tsveto chek 2 Golub'	Boosey	S(T), 2cl, 2fl, pf, st qt
Pribaoutki (Rus/Fr/Ger) 1 Kornilo 2 Natashka 3 Polkovnik' 4 Starets' i zayats'	Chester, 1917	V, bn, cl, db, fl, ob, va, vc, vn
Four Songs 1 The Drake 2 A Russian spiritual 3 Geese and Swans 4 Tilimbom	Chester, 1955	V, fl, gtr, hp
Three Songs from William Shakespeare 1 Musick to heare 2 Full fadom five 3 When Dasies pied	Boosey, 1954	Ms, cl, fl, va

SUBEN, JOEL (1946-   )

Five Goethe Songs	APNM	Bar, gtr, vc

SUSA, CONRAD (1935-   )

Serenade #5	EC Schirmer	TT, ob, perc, vc

SYDEMAN, WILLIAM (1928-   )

Full Circle	Seesaw	SAB, cl, perc, pf(org), trbn, vc
4 Japanese Songs	EC Schirmer	S, 2vn
Jabberwocky (Carroll)	"	S(T), fl, vc
Malediction	Seesaw	T, 4st, tp
3 Songs after Emily Dickinson	EC Schirmer	S(T), vc
3 Songs on Elizabethan Texts	"	S(T), fl

TALMA, LOUISE (1906-   )

All the Days of my Life	AMC	T, cl, perc, pf, vc

TANENBAUM, ELIAS (1924-   )

Fantasies of a Prisoner	ACA	Bar, btrbn, cl, fl, hp, perc, tpt, vc, vn

Images	ACA	fV, perc, pf, tp
Peter Quince at the Clavier	"	S, btrbn, cl, fl/pic, va

TATE, PHYLLIS (1911-   )

Apparitions * 20'	Oxford, 1972	T, harm, pf, st qt
Nocturne (Sidney Keyes) * 25'	Oxford, 1949	STBarB, bcl, cel, db, st qt
A Victorian Garland	Oxford	S, hn, pf

TAVENER, JOHN (1944-   )

Three Surrealist Songs (Lucie-Smith)	Chester	Ms, bongo drums, tp, pf

TAYLOR, CLIFFORD (1923-   )

5	Two Songs (Sandburg)	ACA	S(T), cl, pf

TCHAIKOVSKY, PYOTR IL'YICH (1840-1893)

46	Six Duets	T, 43	
	1 Vecher (I. Surikov)		SMs, pf
	2 Shotlandskaya ballada		SBar, pf
	3 Slyozi (F. Tyutchev)		SMs, pf
	4 Vogorode, vozle brodu (Surikov, aft Shevchenko)		SMs, pf
	5 Minula strast (Tolstoy)		SMs, pf
	6 Rassvet (Surikov)		SMs, pf
	Noch	"	SATB, pf

TELEMANN, GEORG PHILIPP (1681-1767)

Der harmonische Gottesdienst: 72 solo cantatas	T, 2-5	V, bc, inst(fl, ob, rec, vn)

available separately:

Ein Jeder lauft	Bärenreiter	S(T), bc, ob(vn)
Ew'ge Quelle milder Strom	"	medV, bc, fl(vn)
Gott will Mensch und sterblich werden	"	hiV, bc, vn
Hemmet den Eifer	"	hiV, bc, rec
Ihr Völker hört * Christmas	"	S(T), bc, fl
Jauchzet frohlocket * Christmas	Vieweg	medV, bc, vn
Jauchzet, ihr Christen, sei vergnügt	Bärenreiter	S(T), bc, vn
Lauter Wonne, lauter Freude	Hänssler	S, bc, rec
Locke nur	Schott	S, bc, rec
Vor des lichten Tages Schein * Advent	Vieweg	medV, bc, fl

other solo cantatas:

Ach Herr, strafe mich nicht (Psalm 6)	Deutscher, 1967	A, bc, 2vn
Ach Herr, strafe mich nicht (Psalm 6)	Hänssler, 1978	S(T), bc, ob, vn
Alles redet jetzt und singet	Bärenreiter, 1955	SB, bc, 2fl, 2ob, va, 2vn
Der Weiberorden	Deutscher, 1966	S, bc, 2vn
Die Hoffnung ist mein Leben	Bärenreiter, 1954	B, bc, vn
Erquicktes Herz sei voller Freude	Hänssler, 1960 (Die Kantate, 43)	A(B), bc, vn
Gesegnet ist die Zuversicht	Bärenreiter, 1954	TB, bc, 2rec, 2vn
Gottlichs Kind, lass mit Entzucken	Hänssler	ST(MsBar), bc, tpt, vn
Ha ha! wo will wi hut hoch danzen	Deutscher, 1971	S, bc, vn
Ich hebe meine Augen auf den Bergen (Psalm 121)	Hänssler, 1978	T(S), bc, vn
Ich will den Herrn loben allezeit (Psalm 34)	"	S(A)T(B), bc
Jauchzet dem Herrn, alle Welt (Psalm 100)	Hanssler	B, bc, tpt, va, vn
Kanarienvogel Kantate	Bärenreiter, 1952	V, bc, 2fl, va
Laudate pueri Dominum (Psalm 112)	Hänssler, 1981	S(T), bc, 2ob, 2vn
Nicht uns...nur dir allein	Hänssler, 1972	S(T), bc, fl
Süsse Hoffnung, wenn ich frage	Bärenreiter, 1954	T, bc, 2bn, va, 2vn
Weiche, Lust und Fröhlichkeit	Hänssler, 1966 (Die Kantate, 280)	S, bc, ob, va, 2vn
Wohl dem, der den Herrn fürchtet	Hänssler, 1980	2medV, bc
Zerreiss das Herz	Hänssler	S, bc, rec, vc, 2vn

TERZAKIS, DIMITRI (1938-   )

Ethos B (no text)	Gerig	Ms, fl, vc

THOMSON, VIRGIL (1896-   )

Capital Capitals (G. Stein)	Boosey, 1968	TTBB, pf
Collected Poems (Kenneth Koch)	Southern, 1978	SBar, pf
Four songs to poems of Thomas Campion	Ricordi, 1953	Ms, cl, hp, va

1 Follow your Saint
2 There is a Garden in her Face
3 Rose cheek'd Laura, come
4 Follow thy fair son

Stabat Mater	Boosey, 1981	S, st qt

TIPPETT, MICHAEL (1905-   )

Songs for Ariel (Shakespeare)	Schott	medV, cl, fl/pic, hn, hpd, perc

TOGNI, CAMILLO (1922-   )
       Sei Notturni (Trakl)   Zerboni   Ms, cl, 2pf, vn
       * 9'

       Rondeaux per 10 (Charles   "   S, 9inst
         d'Orleans)

TREMBLAY, GILLES (1932-   )
       Kekoba   Berandol   SMsT, ondes
                                          martenot, perc

TRIMBLE, LESTER (1923-   )
       Four Fragments from the   Peters, 1967   hiV, cl, fl, hpd
         Canterbury Tales
       1 Prologe
       2 A Knyght
       3 A Yong Squier
       4 The Wyf of Biside Bathe
       * 17'

       Petit concert   Peters   medV, hpd, ob, vn
       * 12'

TRUNK, RICHARD (1879-1968)
 81   Idylls (Ger/Eng)   Leuckart   SBar, pf

TURINA, JOAQUIN (1882-1914)
       Las nueve musas   UME   V, pf, st qt, vn

TUROK, PAUL (1929-   )
       3 Songs   ACA   S, fl

UNG, CHINARY (1942-   )
       Mohori   Peters   Ms, fl, gtr, hp,
                                          ob, 2perc, pf, vc

       Tall Wind   "   S, fl, gtr, ob, vc

VALLS, MANUEL (1920-   )
       Canciones Sefarditas   UME, 1975   S, fl, gtr

VAUGHAN WILLIAMS, RALPH (1872-1958)
       Along the Field (Housman)   Oxford, 1954   hiV, vn
       1 We'll to the woods no more
       2 Along the field
       3 The Half-moon westers low
       4 In the morning
       5 The Sigh that heaves the
         grasses
       6 Good-Bye
       7 Fancy's knell

        8 With rue my heart is laden

Ten Blake Songs	Oxford, 1958	T(S), ob

        1 Infant joy
        2 A Poison tree
        3 The Piper
        4 London
        5 The Lamb
        6 The Shepherd
        7 Ah! Sun-Flower
        8 Cruelty has a human heart
        9 The Divine Image
       10 Eternity

Two English Folk-Songs	Oxford, 1935	medV, vn

        1 Searching for Lambs
        2 The Lawyer

Four Hymns	Boosey, 1967	T, pf, va

        1 Lord! Come away! (Jeremy
          Taylor)
        2 Who is this fair one? (Isaac
          Watts)
        3 Come love come Lord (Richard
          Crashaw)
        4 Evening Hymn (Robert Bridges)

Merciless Beauty (Chaucer)	Curwen, 1922	S(T), vc, 2vn

        1 Your eyen two
        2 So hath your beauty
        3 Since I from love

On Wenlock Edge (Housman)	Boosey	T, st qt

Three Vocalises	Oxford, 1960	S, cl

        1 Prelude
        2 Scherzo
        3 Quasi menuetto

VERCOE, ELIZABETH (1941-   )

Herstory	AMC	S, pf, vib

VERRALL, JOHN (1908-   )

The Rose of the World	ACA	S, fl, pf

VILLA-LOBOS, HEITOR (1887-1959)

Bachianas Brasileira no. 5	AMP, 1947	S, 8vc
Il Bove (Carducci)	Napoleao (HL)	V, pf, vc
Poema da Criança e Sua Mama	Eschig, 1929	hiV, cl, fl, vc
Suite	Eschig, 1925	V, vn

        1 A Menina e a Cancao
        2 Quéro ser Alégre
        3 Sertaneja

VIVALDI, ANTONIO (1678-1741)
    All'ombra di sospetto   Deutscher, 1970   hiV, bc, fl

VLAD, ROMAN (1919-   )
    Immer wieder (Rilke)   Universal   S, bn, cl, eng hn, hp, mar, pf, va, vc, vib

VLIJMEN, JAN VAN (1935-   )
    Mythos   Donemus   Ms, bn, cl, fl, hn, ob, va, vc, 2vn

VOGEL, WLADIMIR (1896-   )
    Dal Quaderno di Francine Settenne   Zerboni   S, fl, pf

VOLKONSKY, ANDREY MIKHAYLOVICH (1933-   )
    Les Plaintes de Chtchaza   Universal   S, eng hn, hpd, perc, va, vn

WARD-STEINMAN, DAVID (1936-   )
    Fragments from Sappho   Marks   S, cl, fl, pf

WARLOCK, PETER (1894-1930)
    Corpus Christi   Curwen, 1927   ST, st qt

    The Curlew (Yeats)   Stainer, 1924   T, eng hn, fl, st qt

    My Lady is a Pretty One   Oxford, 1956   hiV, st qt

    Sorrow's Lullaby (T. Beddoes)   Oxford, 1927   SBar, st qt

WEBER, BEN (1916-1979)
  20   Four Songs   New Mus Ed   S(T), vc

  29   Concert Aria after Solomon   ACA   S, bn, cl, fl, hn, ob, pf, vc, vn

  48   Three Songs   Bomart   T(S), st qt

WEBERN, ANTON (1883-1945)
  8   Zwei Lieder (Rilke)   Universal, 1926   Ms, cel, cl/bcl, hn, hp, tpt, va, vc, vn
    * 5'

  14   Sechs Lieder (Trakl)   "   S, bcl, cl, vc, vn

  15   Fünf Geistliche Lieder   Universal, 1924   S, cl/bcl, fl, hp, tpt, vn/va

  16   Fünf Canons (Lat)   Universal, 1928   S, bcl, cl

17	Drei Volkstexte	Universal, 1955	S, bcl, cl, vn/va
18	Drei Lieder	Universal, 1928	S, Ebcl, gtr

WEIGL, KARL (1881-1949)

40	5 Songs	ACA	S, st qt
	5 Duets	"	SBar, pf

WEIGL, VALLY (1889-   )

Beyond Time	"	hiV, pf, vn
Dear Earth * 10'	"	Ms(Bar), hn, pf, vc, vn
Do not Awake Me	"	Ms, pf, vn(fl, cl)
Echoes from Poems (Benton) * 12'	"	Ms(Bar), hn(vc), pf, vn(fl)
Songs Beyond Time (Blankner) * 12'	"	hiV, pf, vn(fl)
Songs from No Boundary (Marshall) * 12'	"	Ms, pf, va(cl, vn)
Songs of Remembrance (Dickinson) * 12'	"	Ms, fl(cl), pf(st qt)
Take My Hand (Segal) * 12'	"	Ms, fl(vn), pf

WEILL, KURT (1900-1950)

10	Frauentanz * 7 movements	Universal, 1924	S, bn, cl, fl, hn, va

WEISGALL, HUGO (1912-   )

Fancies and Inventions (Herrick)	Presser, 1974	Bar, cl, fl, pf, va, vc

WEISS, HERMAN (1946-   )

Cantata	APNM	Ms, cl, va, vn
Cantata II	"	Ms, cl, pf, vn
Cantata III * 4 movements	"	SATB, hn, pf, 2vc

WERNICK, RICHARD F. (1934-   )

Haiku of Basho	Presser	S, cl, db, fl, 2perc, pf, tp, vn

A Prayer for Jerusalem	Presser, 1971	Ms, perc
Songs of Remembrance	Presser	Ms, ob

WESTERGAARD, PETER (1931-   )

Cantata 2 (Dylan Thomas)	Ars Viva	B, 10 inst
Cantata 3 (Leda and the Swan) (Yeats)	Schott	Ms, cl, mar, va, vib

WHITTENBERG, CHARLES (1927-   )

Even though the World keeps changing	ACA	Bar, fl, va, vib
Two Dylan Thomas Songs	"	S, fl, pf

WILLIAMS, RONALD RAY (1947-   )

Suite for Six Texts	ASUC, 1974	T, st qt

WILLIAMSON, MALCOLM (1931-   )

The Musicians of Bremen	Weinberger, 1974	CtCtTBarB

WILSON, DONALD M. (1937-   )

Five Haiku	Galaxy, 1967	T, eng hn, gtr, st qt

WINHAM, GODFREY (1934-1975)

The Habit of Perfection * 14'	APNM	S, st qt

WORK, HENRY CLAY (1832-1884)

The Songs of Henry Clay Work	Da Capo, 1974	SATB, pf

    Agnes by the River
    Babylon is Fallen!
    Beautiful rose
    The Buckskin bag of gold
    Come back to the Farm
    "Come home, father!"
    Corporal Schnapps
    Crossing the grand Sierras
    Dad's a millionaire
    The Girls at Home
    God Save the Nation
    Grafted into the army
    Grandfather's Clock
    Kingdom Coming
    Lillie of the Snow-storm
    Little Major
    Marching through Georgia
    Nell is Lost and Found
    No letters from home
    "Now, Moses"

> Poor Kitty Popcorn
> Ring the Bell, Watchman
> Sleeping for the flag
> Song of a thousand years
> Sweet Echo Dell
> The Mystic Veil
> The Ship That Never Returned
> The Song of the Red Man
> The picture on the wall
> Tis finished! or sing
>   Hallelujah
> Uncle Joe's "Hail Columbia!"
> Wake Nicodemus!
> Washington and Lincoln
> Watching for Pa!
> When the "Evening Star" went
>   down
> Who shall rule this American
>   Nation

WRIGHT, MAURICE (1949-   )

Mozartean Constraint	Bomart	S, bn, fl, gtr, vn
Sonnet at Trifling Intervals * 5'	"	S, cl, fl
Think, but Sing, Sweet Love	"	T, tp, perc

WUORINEN, CHARLES (1938-   )

Madrigale Spirituale	ACA	TBar, 2ob, pf, 2vn
Message to Denmark Hill (Howard)	Peters	Bar, fl, pf, vc

WYNER, YEHUDI (1929-   )

Memorial Music	ACA	S, 3fl

XENAKIS, IANNIS (1922-   )

N'shima	Boosey	MsMs, 2hn, 2trbn, vc
Nuits (syllabic text) * 12' * quarter-tone	Salabert	SSSAAATTTBBB

YTTREHUS, ROLV (1926-   )

Angstwagen	ACA, 1971	S, 3 perc
6 Haiku	ACA	S, fl, hp, vc

ZAGWIJN, HENRI (1878-1954)

Die stille Stadt	Donemus	Ms, fl, hp, st tr
Suite Nègre	"	Ms(Bar), bn, cl, fl, hn, ob, pf

ZAHLER, NOEL (1951-   )
        Three Songs   APNM   Ms, cl, fl, hn, hp,
                                                         ob, perc, tpt, va,
                                                         vc, vn

ZAIMONT, JUDITH (1945-   )
        A Woman of Valor   ACA   Ms, st qt

ZALLMAN, ARLENE (1934-   )
        Songs from Quasimodo   APNM   S, afl, pf, vc

ZENDER, HANS (1936-   )
        3 Rondel nach Mallarmé   Bote   A, fl, va

ZIFRIN, MARILYN J. (1926-   )
        Haiku   ACA   S, hpd, va

ZILCHER, HERMANN (1881-1948)
    52   Marienlieder   Breitkopf   hiV, st qt

    65   Rokoko Suite   "   hiV, pf, vc, vn

ZUCKERMAN, MARK (1948-   )
        Twilight Songs   Bomart   S, fl
        * 7'

BIBLIOGRAPHY

Anderson, E. Ruth. Contemporary American Composers: A Bibliographical
  Dictionary. Second Edition. Boston: G.K. Hall & Co., 1982.

Boyd, Jack Arthur. "Secular Music for the Solo Vocal Ensemble in the
  Nineteenth Century." Ph.D. diss., University of Iowa, 1971.

Cohen, Aaron I. International Encyclopedia of Women Composers. New York and
  London: R.R. Bowker Co., 1981.

Emmons, Shirlee and Sonntag, Stanley. The Art of the Song Recital. New York:
  Schirmer Books, 1979.

Farrish, Margaret K. String Music in Print. New York: R.R. Bowker Co., 1965.

Nardone, Thomas R., ed. Classical Vocal Music in Print. Philadelphia:
  Music-data, Inc., 1976.

Opperman, Kalmen. Repertory of the Clarinet. New York: Ricordi, 1960.

Sadie, Stanley, ed. The New Grove Dictionary of Music and Musicians. London:
  Macmillan Publishers Ltd., 1980.

Solow, Linda I. The Boston Composer's Project. Cambridge: The MIT Press,
  1983.

Tompson, Oscar, ed. International Cyclopedia of Music and Musicians.
  New York: Dodd, Mead & Co., 1975.

Vester, Frans. Flute Repertoire Catalogue. London: Musica Rara, 1967.

Vinton, John, ed. Dictionary of Contemporary Music. New York: E.P. Dutton
  Co., 1974.

MUSIC SOURCES

Although addresses of publishers and their American agents are listed, it is
always more efficient to order music through your own local store.

CODE	COLLECTIONS, LIBRARIES, PUBLISHERS	AMERICAN AGENT
A	Schein, Werke, ed. Adrio (Kassel, 1963-)	
A-R Ed	A-R Editions, Inc. 315 West Gorham Street Madison, WI 53703	
ACA	American Composers' Alliance 170 West 74th Street New York, NY 10023	
AD	Dvorak, Works, ed. Sourek (Prague, 1955-)	
AFMS	Grainger, American Folk-music Settings	
Albert	J. Albert & Son Pty. Ltd. 139 King Street Sydney, N.S.W. Australia 2000	Belwin
Allans	Allans Music Australia Ltd. Box 513J, G.P.O. Melbourne 3001 Australia	
Alsbach	G. Alsbach & Co. P.O. Box 338 NL-1400 AH Bussum Netherlands	Peters
AMBC	Alte Meister des Bel Canto (Frankfurt, New York, C.F. Peters, 1912-27)	
AMC	American Music Center 250 West 57th Street New York, NY 10019	

AME	American Music Edition 263 East Seventh Street New York, NY 10009	C Fischer
AMP	Associated Music Publishers 866 Third Avenue New York, NY 10022	
APNM	Association for the Promotion of New Music 2002 Central Avenue Ship Bottom, NJ 08008	
Arcadia	Arcadia Music Publishing Co., Ltd. P.O. Box 1 Rickmansworth Herts WD3 3AZ England	
Arno	Arno Press 3 Park Avenue New York, NY 10016	
Arrow	Arrow Press	Boosey
Ars Viva	Ars Viva Verlag Weihergarten D-6500 Mainz 1 Germany	Eur Am Mus
Artia	Artia Prag Ve Smeckach 30 Praha 2 Czechoslovakia	Boosey
Ashdown	Edwin Ashdown Ltd.	Music-Eng
ASUC	American Society of University Composers Journal of Music Scores	Eur Am Mus
Augener	Augener Ltd. 18 Great Marlborough Street London W1, England	EC Schirmer
Bärenreiter	Bärenreiter Verlag Heinrich Schütz Alee 31-37 Postfach 100329 D-3500 Kassel-Wilhelmshöhe Germany	Magnamusic
Baron	M. Baron Co. P.O. Box 149 Oyster Bay, NY 11771	
Barry	Barry & Cia Talcahuano 860, Bajo B Buenos Aires 1013-Cap. Federal Argentina	Boosey

Belmont	Belmont Music Publishers P.O. Box 49961 Los Angeles, CA 90049	
Belwin	Belwin-Mills Publishing Corp. 25 Deshon Drive Melville, NY 11747	
Benjamin	Anton J. Benjamin Werderstrasse 44 Postfach 2561 D-2000 Hamburg 13 Germany	AMP
Berandol	Berandol Music Ltd. 11 St. Joseph Street Toronto, Ontario M4Y 1JB Canada	
BFMS	Grainger, British Folk-music Settings	
Bieler	Edmund Bieler Musikverlag Thürmchenswall 72 D-5000 Köln 1 Germany	
Boelke-Bomart	Boelke-Bomart Music Publications Hillsdale, NY 12529	Jerona
Böhm	Anton Böhm & Sohn Postfach 110369 Lange Gasse 26 D-8900 Augsburg 11 Germany	
Bomart	Bomart Music Publications	Boelke-Bomart
Bongiovanni	Casa Musicale Francesco Bongiovanni Via Rizzoli 28E I-40125 Bologna Italy	
Boosey	Boosey & Hawkes, Inc. 200 Smith Street CSB6 Farmingdale, NY 11735	
Bosse	Gustav Bosse Verlag Von der Tann Strasse 38 Postfach 417 D-8400 Regensburg 1 Germany	Magnamusic Eur Am Mus
Bote	Bote & Bock Hardenbergstrasse 9A D-1000 Berlin 12 Germany	AMP
Boyd	See Bibliography	

BPL   Boston Public Library, Boston, MA

Breitkopf-L   Breitkopf & Härtel   A Broude
                        Karlstrasse 10
                        DDR-7010 Leipzig
                        Germany

Breitkopf-W   Breitkopf & Härtel   AMP
                        Walkmühlstrasse 52
                        Postfach 1707
                        D-6200 Wiesbaden 1
                        Germany

Brodt   Brodt Music Co.
                        P.O. Box 9345
                        Charlotte, NC 28299-9345

Broekmans   Broekmans & Van Poppel
                        Badhoevelaan 78
                        NL-1171 DE Badhoevedorp
                        Netherlands

A Broude   Alexander Broude, Inc.
                        575 Eighth Avenue
                        New York, NY 10018

Broude Bros   Broude Brothers Ltd.
                        141 White Oaks Road
                        Williamstown, MA 02167

Bruzzichelli   Aldo Bruzzichelli, Editore   Margun
                        Lungarno Guicciardini 27r
                        I-50124 Firenze
                        Italy

BW   Brahms, Werke, ed. Gal and
                           Mandyczewski (Leipzig, 1926-7)

C   Couperin, Oeuvres complètes, ed.
                           M. Cauchie and others (Paris, 1933)

C   Dargomïzhsky, Complete Collection of
(Dargomïzshky)   Vocal Ensembles and Choruses, ed.
                           M.K. Pekelis (Moscow and Leningrad,
                           1950)

Carisch   Carisch S.p.A.   Boosey
                        Via General Fara, 39
                        Casella Postale 10170
                        I-20124 Milano
                        Italy

Catamount   Bennington, Vermont

CeBeDeM   Centre Belge de Documentation Musicale   H Elkan
                        rue d'Arlon 75-77
                        B-1040 Bruxelles
                        Belgium

CEN	Casa Editrice Nazionalmusic	
Chappell	Chappell & Co., Inc. 810 Seventh Avenue New York, NY 10019	Leonard
Chester	J. &. W. Chester, Ltd. Chester Music-Edition Wilhelm Hansen 7-9 Eagle Court London EC1M 5QD England	A Broude Magnamusic
Choudens	Edition Choudens 38, rue Jean Mermoz F-75008 Paris France	Baron Elkan-Vogel Peters
Colombo	Franco Colombo Publications	Belwin
Concordia	Concordia Publishing House 3558 South Jefferson Avenue St. Louis, MO 63118	
Cramer	J.B. Cramer & Co., Ltd. 99 St. Martin's Lane London WC2N 4AZ England	Brodt
Curwen	J. Curwen & Sons	G Schirmer
Czech	Czechoslovak Music Information Centre Besedni 3 CS-118 00 Praha 1 Czechoslovakia	Boosey
Da Capo	Da Capo Press, Inc. 233 Spring Street New York, NY 10013	
De Santis	Edizioni de Santis Viale Mazzini, 6 I-00195 Roma Italy	
Deiro	Pietro Deiro Publications 133 Seventh Avenue South New York, NY 10014	
Deutscher	Deutscher Verlag für Musik Postschliessfach 147 Karlstrasse 10 DDR-7010 Leipzig Germany	A Broude
DFMS	Grainger, Danish Folk-music Settings	

Doblinger	Ludwig Doblinger Verlag Dorotheergasse 10 A-1011 Wien Austria	AMP
Donemus	Donemus Foundation Paulus Potterstraat 14 NL-1071 CZ Amsterdam Netherlands	Presser
Dreiklang	Dreiklang-Dreimasken Buhnen und Musikverlag D-8000 München Germany	Orlando
Drustvo	Edicije Drustva Slovenskih Skladateljev Trg Francoske Revolucije 6 YU-6100 Ljubljana Yugoslavia	
DTO	Denkmäler der Tonkunst in Osterreich	
Durand	Durand & Cie 21, rue Vernet F-75008 Paris France	Elkan-Vogel
Ear Mus Fac	Early Music Facsimiles P.O. Box 1813 Ann Arbor, MI 48106	
Ed Fr Mus	Editions Françaises de Musique 115 Rue de Bac F-75007 Paris France	Presser
Edi-Pan	Edi-Pan	De Santis
EDM	Das Erbe deutscher Musik (Leipzig, Breitkopf & Härtel, 1935-)	
Elkan-Vogel	Elkan-Vogel, Inc. Presser Place Bryn Mawr, PA 19010	
H Elkan	Henri Elkan Music Publisher 2019 Walnut Street Philadelphia, PA 19103	
Enoch	Enoch & Cie 27 Boulevard des Italiens F-75002 Paris France	AMP Baron Brodt Peer

Eschig	Editions Max Eschig 48 rue de Rome F-75008 Paris France	AMP
Eulenburg	Edition Eulenburg 305 Bloomfield Avenue Nutley, NJ 07110	
Eur Am Mus	European American Music Dist. Corp. 11 West End Road Totowa, NJ 07512	
Faber	Faber Music Ltd. 3 Queen Street London WC1N 3AU England	G Schirmer
C Fischer	Carl Fischer, Inc. 56-62 Cooper Square New York, NY 10003	
J Fischer	J. Fischer & Bro.	Belwin
FMA	Florilegium Musicae Antiquae	Hänssler
Fog	Dan Fog Musikforlag Grabrodretorv 7 DK-1154 Kobenhavn K Denmark	Peters
Forni	Arnaldo Forni Editore Via Gramsci 164 I-40010 Sala Bolognese Italy	
Foster	Mark Foster Music Co. 28 East Springfield Avenue P.O. Box 4012 Champaign, IL 61820-1312	
Fürstner	Fürstner Ltd.	Boosey
G (Buxtehude)	Buxtehude, Werke, ed. Gurlitt (Klecken and Hamburg, 1925-58)	
G (Glinka)	Glinka, Polnoye sobraniye sochineniy, ed. V. Ya Shebalin and others (Moscow, 1955-69)	
GA (Beethoven)	Beethoven, Werke (Leipzig, 1862-5)	
GA (Loewe)	Loewe, Werke, ed. Runze (Leipzig, 1899-1904)	
Galaxy	Galaxy Music Corp. 131 West 86th Street New York, NY 10024	

General   General Music Publishing Co., Inc.
                   145 Palisade Street
                   Dobbs Ferry, NY 10522

Gerig   Musikverlag Hans Gerig   Breitkopf-W
                   Drususgasse 7-11   MCA
                   D-5000 Köln 1
                   Germany

Gregg   Gregg International Publishers, Ltd.
                   1 Westmead, Farnborough
                   Hants GU14 7RU
                   England

H   Cornelius, Werke, ed. M. Hasse
                      (Leipzig, 1905-6)

Hamelle   Hamelle & Cie   Elkan-Vogel
                   175 rue Saint-Honoré
                   F-75040 Paris Cedex 01
                   France

Hansen   Edition Wilhelm Hansen   A Broude

Hänssler   Hänssler-Verlag   Foster
                   Bismarckstrasse 4
                   Postfach 1220
                   D-7303 Neuhausen-Stuttgart
                   Germany

Henle   G. Henle Verlag
                   Forstenrieder Allee 122
                   Postfach 71 04 66
                   D-8000 München 71
                   Germany

Heugel   Heugel & Cie   Presser
                   175 rue Saint-Honoré
                   F-75040 Paris Cedex 01
                   France

HG   Handel, Werke, ed. Chrysander (Leipzig
                      and Bergedorf bei Hamburg, 1858-94,
                      1902/R1965)

Hinshaw   Hinshaw Music, Inc.
                   P.O. Box 470
                   Chapel Hill, NC 27514

HL   Edna Kuhn Loeb Music Library, Harvard
                      University, Cambridge, MA

HMA   Harvard Musical Association, Boston, MA

Houghton   Houghton Library, Harvard University,
                      Cambridge, MA

HS   Beethoven, Sämtliche Werke: Supplemente,
                      ed. W. Hess (Wiesbaden, 1959-71)

Hug   Hug & Co.
                   Limmatqual 26
                   CH-8022 Zurich
                   Switzerland

HW   Haydn, <u>Werke</u>, ed. J. Haydn-Institut
                      (Munich, 1958-)

International   International Music Co.
                   437 Fifth Avenue
                   New York, NY 10016

Ione   Ione Press   EC Schirmer

Isr Mus Inst   Israel Music Institute
                   P.O. Box 11253
                   Tel-Aviv 61 112
                   Israel

Israeli   Israeli Music Publications, Inc.   Presser
                   P.O. Box 7681
                   Jerusalem 91076
                   Israel

Jerona   Jerona Music Corp.
                   81 Trinity Place
                   Hackensack, NY 07601

Jobert   Editions Jean Jobert   Presser
                   76, rue Quincampoix
                   F-75003 Paris
                   France

Kalmus   Edwin F. Kalmus
                   Miami-Dade Industrial Park
                   P.O. Box 1007
                   Opa Locka, FL 33054

A Kalmus   Alfred A. Kalmus Ltd.
                   38 Eldon Way, Paddock Wood
                   Tonbridge, Kent TN12 6BE
                   England

Kerby   E.C. Kerby Ltd.
                   198 Davenport Road
                   Toronto, Ontario M5R 1J2
                   Canada

Kistner   Fr. Kistner & C.F.W. Siegel & Co.   Concordia
                   Adrian-Kiels-Strasse 2
                   D-5000 Köln 90
                   Germany

Kultura   Editio Musica Budapest   Boosey
                   H-1389 Budapest 62   Presser

Kunzelmann   Edition Kunzelmann-U.S.A.
                   305 Bloomfield Avenue
                   Nutley, NJ 07110

LC	Library of Congress, Washington, DC	
Leduc	Alphonse Leduc 175 rue Saint-Honore F-75040 Paris Cedex 01 France	Baron Brodt
Leeds	Leeds Music Ltd. MCA Building 2450 Victoria Park Avenue Willowdale, Ontario M2J 4A2 Canada	Belwin
Lemoine	Henry Lemoine & Cie 17, rue Pigalle F-75009 Paris France	Presser
Leonard	Hal Leonard Music 8112 West Bluemound Road Milwaukee, WI 53213	
Leuckart	F.E.C. Leuckart Nibelungenstrasse 48 D-8000 Munchen 19 Germany	AMP
Lienau	Robert Lienau, Musikverlag Lankwitzerstrasse 9 D-1000 Berlin 45 Germany	
M	Monteverdi, *Tutte le opere*, ed. Malipiero (Asolo, 1926-42)	
Magnamusic	Magnamusic-Baton, Inc. 10370 Page Industrial Boulevard St. Louis, MO 63132	
Margun	Margun Music, Inc. 167 Dudley Road Newton Centre, MA 02159	
Marks	Edward B. Marks Music Corp. 1619 Broadway New York, NY 10019	Leonard
MCA	MCA and Mills/MCA Joint Venture Editions 445 Park Avenue New York, NY 10022	Belwin
McGinnis	McGinnis & Marx P.O. Box 229, Planetarium Station New York, NY 10024	Deiro
Media	Media Press P.O. Box 250 Elwyn, PA 19063	

Mercury	Mercury Music Corp.	Presser
Merion	Merion Music, Inc.	Presser
Merrymount	Merrymount Music, Inc.	Presser
Merseburger	Merseburger Verlag Motzstrasse 13 D-3500 Kassel Germany	Magnamusic
Mez Kniga	Soviet State	G Schirmer
Mills	Mills Music Jewish Catalogue	Transcon
Mobart	Mobart Music Publications	Boelke-Bomart
Modern	Edition Modern Musikverlag Hans Wewerka Elisabethstrasse 38 D-8000 München 40 Germany	
Moeck	Hermann Moeck Verlag Postfach 143 D-3100 Celle 1 Germany	Eur Am Mus
Möseler	Karl Heinrich Möseler Verlag Hoffman-von-Fallersleben-Strasse 8-10 Postfach 1460 D-3340 Wolfenbüttel Germany	Magnamusic
Müller	Willy Müller, Süddeutscher Musikverlag Marzgasse 5 D-6900 Heidelberg Germany	
Music-Eng	Music Sales Ltd. 78 Newman Street London W1P 3LA England	
Musica Rara	Musica Rara Le Traversier Chemin de la Buire F-84170 Monteux France Musica Rara, U.S.A. 305 Bloomfield Avenue Nutley, NJ 07110	
Muzgiz	Soviet State	G Schirmer
Muzyka	Soviet State	G Schirmer

N	Schütz, <u>Werke</u>, ed. Graulich and others (Kassel, 1955-)	
Nagels	Nagels Verlag	AMP Magnamusic
NBE	Berlioz, <u>New Berlioz Edition</u>, ed. Macdonald (Kassel, 1967-)	
NEC	Harriet M. Spaulding Library, The New England Conservatory of Music, Boston, MA	
New Mus Ed	New Music Edition	Presser
NMA	Mozart, <u>Werke</u>, ed. Schmid, Plath and Rehm (Kassel, 1955-)	
Nordiska	AB Nordiska Musikförlaget Edition Wilhelm Hansen Box 745, Warfvinges Vag 32 S-100 30 Stockholm Sweden	A Broude Magnamusic
Norsk	Norsk Musikforlag AS Karl Johansgaten 39 P.O. Box 1499 Vika, Oslo Norway	Magnamusic
Novello	Novello & Co., Ltd. Fairfield Road Borough Green Sevenoaks, Kent TN15 8DT England	Presser
NSA	Schubert, <u>Neue Ausgabe sämtlicher Werke</u>, ed. Durr, Feil, Landon and others (Kassel, 1964-)	
NYPL	New York Public Library, New York, NY	
OC	Rameau, <u>Oeuvres complètes</u>, ed. Saint-Saens, <u>Malherbe</u> (Paris, 1895-1924/ R1968)	
OEPM	Grainger, <u>Settings and Songs and Tunes from William Chappell's 'Old English Popular Music'</u>	
L'Oiseau	Editions de L'Oiseau-Lyre Les Remparts Boite Postale 515 MC-98015 Monaco Cedex	
Orlando	Orlando Musikverlag Kaprunerstrasse 11 D-8000 München 21 Germany	

Oxford	Oxford University Press 37 Dover Street London W1X 4AH England
	Oxford University Press 1600 Pollitt Drive Fair Lawn, NJ 07410
Panton	Panton Ricni 12 CS-118 39 Praha 1 Czechoslovakia
Peer	Peer International Corp. 1740 Broadway New York, NY 10019
Penn State	Pennsylvania State University Press 215 Wagner Building University Park, PA 16802
Peters	Edition Peters C.F. Peters Corp. 373 Park Avenue South New York, NY 10016
Presser	Theodore Presser Co. Presser Place Bryn Mawr, PA 19010
Prowse	Keith Prowse Music Publishing Co. 138-140 Charing Cross Road London, WC2H OLD England
PS	Purcell, Works, The Purcell Society (London, 1878-1965; rev2/1961-)
PWM	Polskie Wydawnictwo Muzyczne Al. Krasinskiego 11a PL-31-111 Krakow Poland
QR	Rossini, Quaderni Rossiniani (Pesaro, 1954-)
R	Reger, Werke (Wiesbaden, 1954-)
Rarities	Rarities for Strings Publications 11300 Juniper Drive University Circle Cleveland, OH 44106
Recital Pub	Recital Publications, Ltd. P.O. Box 1697 Huntsville, TX 77340

Ricordi   G. Ricordi & Co.   G Schirmer
                   Via Berchet 2
                   Milano
                   Italy

RK   Rimsky-Korsakov, Polnoye sobraniye
                       sochineniy (Complete works) ed.
                       A. Rimsky-Korsakov and others
                       (Moscow, 1946-70)

RMTB   Grainger, Room-music Tit-bits

Rouart   Rouart-Lerolle & Cie   G Schirmer

Row   R.D. Row Music Co.   C Fischer

S (Buxtehude)   Buxtehude, Abendmusiken und Kirchen-
                       kantaten, ed. M. Seiffert, DDT, xiv
                       (1903, rev. 2/1957 by H.J. Moser)

S (Grainger)   Grainger, Sentimentals

Salabert   Francis Salabert Editions   G Schirmer
                   22 rue Chauchat
                   F-75009 Paris
                   France

Schauer   Richard Schauer, Music Publishers   AMP
                   67 Belsize Lane, Hampstead
                   London NW3 5AX
                   England

EC Schirmer   E.C. Schirmer Music Co.
                   112 South Street
                   Boston, MA 02111

G Schirmer   G. Schirmer, Inc.
                   866 Third Avenue
                   New York, NY 10022

Schlesinger   EC Schirmer

Schott   Schott & Co. Ltd.   Eur Am Mus
                   48 Great Marlborough Street
                   London W1V 2BN
                   England

B Schott   B. Schotts Söhne   Eur Am Mus
                   Weihergarten 5
                   Postfach 3640
                   D-6500 Mainz
                   Germany

Seesaw   Seesaw Music Corp.
                   2067 Broadway
                   New York, NY 10023

Senart   Ed. Maurice Senart   G Schirmer
                   22 rue Chauchat

	F-75009 Paris France	
Sheppard	John Sheppard Music Press	Eur Am Mus
Sikorski	Hans Sikorski Verlag Johnsallee 23 Postfach 132001 D-2000 Hamburg 13 Germany	G Schirmer
Simrock	Nicholas Simrock Lyra House 37 Belsize Lane London NW3 England	AMP
Sirius	Sirius-Verlag	Peters
Sonzogno	Casa Musicale Sonzogno Via Bigli 11 I-20121 Milano Italy	Belwin
Southern	Southern Music Publishing Co., Inc.	Peer
Southern Peer	Southern Music Publishing Co., Inc.	Peer
Stainer	Stainer & Bell Ltd. 82 High Road East Finchley London N2 9PW England	Galaxy
Stim	STIMs informationcentral för Svensky Musik (Swedish Music Information Center) Birger Jarlsgatan 6 B S-102 42 Stockholm Sweden	
Supraphon	Supraphon Pulackeho 1 CS-112 99 Praha Czechoslovakia	
SW	Schumann, *Werke*, ed. C. Schumann, J. Brahms and others (Leipzig, 1881-93)	
Swan	Swan & Co. P.O. Box 1 Rickmansworth, Herts WD3 3AZ England	Arcadia
T (Tchaikovsky)	Tchaikovsky, *Polnoye sobraniye sochineniy* (Moscow and Leningrad, 1940-71)	

T (Telemann)	Telemann, <u>Werke</u>, (Kassel and Basle, 1950-)	
Tonger	P.J. Tonger, Musikverlag Auf dem Brand 3 Postfach 501865 D-5000 Köln-Rodenkirchen 50 Germany	
Tonos	Editions Tonos Ahastrasse 7 D-6100 Darmstadt Germany	Seesaw
Transat	Editions Musicales Transatlantiques 50, rue Joseph-de-Maistre F-75018 Paris France	Presser
Transcon	Transcontinental Music Publications 838 Fifth Avenue New York, NY 10021	
Tri-ten	Tritone Press and Tenuto Publications P.O. Box 5081, Southern Station Hattiesburg, MS 39401	Presser
UME	Union Musical Espanola Carrera de San Jeronimo 26 Madrid Spain	AMP
Univ Mus Ed	University Music Editions P.O. Box 192-Ft. George Station New York, NY 10040	
Universal	Universal Edition Bösendorfer Strasse 12 Postfach 130 A-1015 Wien Austria	Eur Am Mus
Vieweg	Chr. Friedrich Vieweg, Musikverlag Nibelungenstrasse 48 D-8000 München 19 Germany	AMP
Viking	Viking Press, Inc. 625 Madison Avenue New York, NY 10022	
Waterloo	Waterloo Music Co., Ltd. 3 Regina Street North Waterloo, Ontario N2J 4A5 Canada	
Weinberger	Josef Weinberger Ltd. 12-14 Mortimer Street	AMP Boosey

	London W1N 8EL	Marks
	England	G Schirmer
Zanibon	G. Zanibon Edition Piazza dei Signori, 44 I-35100 Padova Italy	
Zerboni	Edizioni Suvini Zerboni Via Quintiliano 40 I-20138 Milano Italy	Boosey
Zimmermann	Wilhelm Zimmermann, Musikverlag Gaugrafenstrasse 19-23 D-6000 Frankfurt-am-Main Germany	G Schirmer

INDEX

This index is by scoring, with voices in score order, followed by instruments in alphabetical order. The composers' names which follow indicate the location of works with that scoring.

S, afl, bn, btrbn, fl, 4perc, vc, vn BENTON
S, afl, cl, pf, tp, va, vc IVEY
S, afl, db OGDON
S, afl, pf, vc ZALLMAN
S, amp hn, cl, db, fl, hp, perc, pf, vc, 2vn BOESMANS
S, asax, bn BLACHER
S, asax, pf, tpt, trbn, vc, vn ANDERSON
S, bc, bn, fl, ob, timp, tpt, vn CLERAMBAULT
S, bc, bn, 3vn BUXTEHUDE
S, bc, fl CAMPRA, HANDEL, A. SCARLATTI
S, bc, fl, vn CLERAMBAULT
S, bc, 2fl(2vn) CACCINI
S, bc, 2fl, vn COUPERIN
S, bc, gam RAMEAU
S, bc, gam, vn BUXTEHUDE
S, bc, gam, 2vn BUXTEHUDE
S, bc, 2gam ROSENMULLER
S, bc, ob, va, 2vn TELEMANN
S, bc, rec TELEMANN
S, bc, 2rec, 2vn BOXBERG
S, bc, rec, vc, 2vn TELEMANN
S, bc, 2st BUXTEHUDE
S, bc, 4st BUXTEHUDE
S, bc, tpt, 2vn A. SCARLATTI
S, bc, va, vle, 2vn BUXTEHUDE
S, bc, va, 2vn PERGOLESI
S, bc, vle, 2vn BUXTEHUDE
S, bc, vn BUXTEHUDE, COUPERIN, HUNFF, TELEMANN
S, bc, vn(fl) BERNIER, CAMPRA
S, bc, 2vn BERNHARD, BUXTEHUDE, CALDARA, KRIEGER, LEO, ROSENMULLER, A. SCARLATTI, SCHUTZ, TELEMANN
S, bc, ob(vn), 2vn BERNHARD
S, bcl, bn, cl, fl FELDMAN
S, bcl, cl WEBERN

S, bcl, cl, fl, perc, trbn, vib LANZA
S, bcl, cl, hp, tpt, trbn, va, va, vn STEARNS
S, bcl, cl, vc, vn WEBERN
S, bcl, cl, vn/va WEBERN
S, bcl, db, fl, perc, pf(cel), va, vc, vn MYROW
S, bcl, fl, hn, hp, vn FORTNER
S, bcl, fl, hp, ob, perc, va, vc, 2vn R. MALIPIERO
S, bcl, fl, vc, vn STOCK
S, bcl, fl, vn BENTON
S, bcl, hp, tpt, va HOPKINS
S, bells, hp, 4perc, vib BOULEZ
S, bfl(treb rec), 2perc, sitar CRUMB
S, bn BLANK
S, bn, cel, cl, fl, hn, hp, ob, perc, va STOUT
S, bn, cl, db, fl, hn, ob d'am DIEPENBROCK
S, bn, cl, db, fl, hp, va BLISS
S, bn, cl, eng hn, hp, mar, pf, va, vc, vib VLAD
S, bn, cl, fl, hn, ob DIEPENBROCK
S, bn, cl, fl(pic), hn, ob, perc, pf, tpt, trbn CHOU
S, bn, cl, fl, hn, ob/eng hn, pf FROIDEBISE
S, bn, cl, fl, hn, ob, pf, tpt MONOD
S, bn, cl, fl, hn, ob, pf, tpt, trbn SALVIUCCI
S, bn, cl, fl, hn, ob, pf, vc, vn WEBER
S, bn, cl, fl, hn, ob, vn EL-DABH
S, bn, cl, fl, hn, va WEILL
S, bn, cl, fl, hp, ob ARIOSTI
S, bn, cl, fl, hp, ob, pf, tpt, trbn, va, vc, vn DALLAPICCOLA
S, bn, cl, fl, ob, perc, st PORTER
S, bn, cl, fl, ob, pf, st qt DELAGE